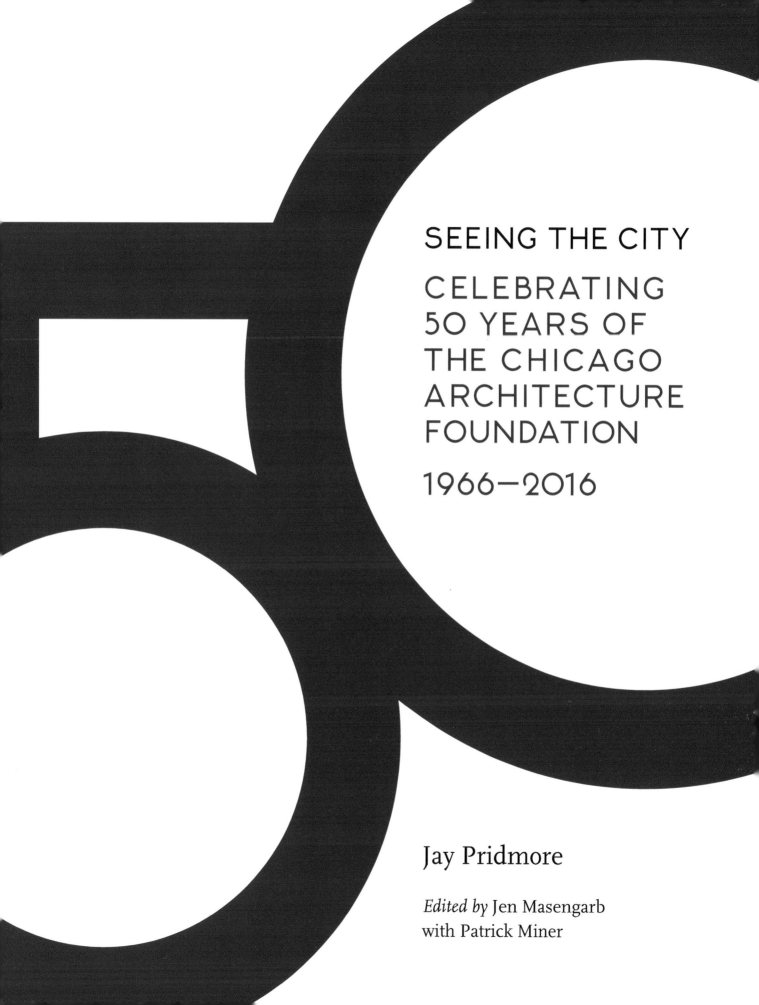

SEEING THE CITY

CELEBRATING 50 YEARS OF THE CHICAGO ARCHITECTURE FOUNDATION

1966–2016

Jay Pridmore

Edited by Jen Masengarb
with Patrick Miner

*Seeing the City: Celebrating 50 Years
of the Chicago Architecture Foundation, 1966–2016*
Jay Pridmore

Design and Production: Jena Sher Graphic Design
Editors: Jen Masengarb with Patrick Miner
Image curation, research and captions: Jen Masengarb

Typefaces: CAF Type, Avenir, FF Scala
Printer: Best Imaging Solutions, Inc.

Front cover photo: Chicago model at the Chicago
Architecture Foundation (Marko Dumlija, 2016)

Inside cover photo: Students explore the Chicago
model at the Chicago Architecture Foundation
(Anne Evans, 2009)

Inside back cover photo: Docent Charles McLaughlin
(class of 2008) leads a CAF River Cruise aboard
Chicago's First Lady Cruises (Courtesy Chicago's
First Lady Cruises, 2015)

Printed in the United States of America.
ISBN 978-0-9973615-0-6
First Printing, June 2016

Jay Pridmore is a journalist and author who has
written many books about architecture, including
a longtime favorite at the CAF store, *Chicago
Architecture and Design* (Abrams 1993, 2005).

This book was made possible by the generous support
of The Richard H. Driehaus Foundation.

CONTENTS

FOREWORD

I often wonder if the founders of the Chicago Architecture Foundation (CAF) ever imagined what the organization might look like in 2016. If they did, I'm sure they would be pleased to know that, because of CAF, the public—both here in Chicago and around the world—is more interested than ever in architecture's past, present, and future. Today, CAF is not only one of Chicago's leading cultural institutions, it is recognized around the world for its interpretation of the built environment.

CAF owes a great deal to the organization's founders—for their conviction that design does matter. In 1966, the founders recognized the important design lessons of architect H.H. Richardson's Glessner House, as well as Chicago's unique role in the development of the skyscraper. Today, we use Chicago as a wider lens, in order to help the public understand why design matters in their own communities. We recognize that a well-designed, healthy and livable city has the power to transform the lives of its citizens.

Among the founders' many seminal initiatives at CAF, one stands out in particular. In 1971, Marian Despres and others conceived a program that would train volunteers to teach the public about Chicago's incomparable architecture. As the docent program developed and the corps of volunteers grew, it also infused CAF with a unique culture—the docents are passionate, generous and extremely knowledgeable advocates and educators who love sharing the city's architecture. Without the docents, with whom CAF is so deeply identified, the Chicago Architecture Foundation would look nothing like it does today.

When I arrived at CAF in 1996, the organization was on its way to becoming as multi-dimensioned as it is today, but its scale and vision were smaller. Since that time, CAF and its impact has grown, along with the public's understanding of the built environment. Through the tireless work of docents, staff, volunteers and our board of trustees we have expanded CAF's influence through an unparalleled array of activities, including: dozens of different tours, exhibitions, lectures, adult courses and Chicago's largest city-wide festival, Open House Chicago. We are also extremely proud of our national leadership in K-12 design education, which includes curricula and workshops to give educators the tools for using architecture to teach core academic subjects. Our teen programs empower youth to apply the design process to real-world problems in their communities, in order to gain transferable skills and become more engaged citizens.

CAF is now serving 650,000 people annually and the organization has been honored in many ways. In 2012, *U.S. News and World Report* named CAF the "#1 best thing to do in Chicago." In 2015, TripAdvisor users named the Chicago Architecture Foundation River Cruise aboard Chicago's First Lady Cruises one of the "top 10 tours in the United States." All three of CAF's curricula and digital tools for K-12 teachers and students have received national awards from the American Institute of Architects. In 2014, the organization was honored to receive the prestigious Keystone Award from the American Architectural Foundation.

As we pass the half-century mark, CAF faces another pivotal moment in our history. For many years CAF has leveraged the built environment of Chicago to teach about architecture, design and civic engagement. Now, after extensive growth, it's time to make a transition and have our own building that captures the culture, spirit and passion of our docents, volunteers, staff and guests. The next era of CAF history will take place in a new Chicago Architecture Center, a permanent home for CAF. Our comprehensive strategic plan has laid the groundwork for expanding our adult and youth engagement strategy. We have strengthened our partnership with Chicago Public Schools to develop STEM-based (science, technology, engineering and math) programs for high school students and piloted innovative programs to attract middle school students, girls in particular, to STEM. We are also developing community initiatives throughout the city to help people engage with civic issues, to better understand their built environment and then to advocate for local change. The new Center will allow CAF to expand the *Chicago Model* where docents can start their tours. We will add permanent exhibitions that tell the story of Chicago innovation and the skyscraper, new spaces for public dialogue and most exciting of all—expanded studio and classroom spaces where students can learn the skills to become design thinkers and affect change in their own communities.

Since 1966, we have seen the public become increasingly hungry for information about the built environment. We now embark on our second 50 years with the expectation that our future—and the future of design education—is every bit as bright as the past.

Lynn J. Osmond, Hon. AIA
President and CEO

ACKNOWLEDGMENTS

Fifty years seems like a long time for most stories. Yet the remarkable growth of the Chicago Architecture Foundation (CAF) has filled almost each one of those years so full that it seems like a short journey from CAF's earliest years to its position today as one of Chicago's largest cultural institutions. For that reason, telling its story and weaving together the stories of so many individuals and ideas represented a challenge that required the assistance of many people.

This history began as a group effort and was created in the same spirit that drives CAF at large—one of collaboration, generosity and passion. Lynn Osmond, CAF president and CEO; Marilyn Jackson, vice president of marketing; Jen Masengarb, director of interpretation and research; Patrick Miner, director of marketing operations; and Marko Dumlija, research intern, were all critical in project management, in telling their stories or in pointing the author in the direction of many others. The project faced a daunting schedule, and our designer Jena Sher created brilliant graphic content simultaneously with the text. Allison Leake, senior graphic designer provided images from CAF's voluminous digital photo archive.

Among the many discussions and interviews conducted for this history were those taken from CAF's founders: Wayne Benjamin, Wilbert Hasbrouck, Dirk Lohan, Paul Lurie and Ben Weese. Our friends at the Glessner House Museum were incredibly helpful, including executive director William Tyre, who provided much needed perspective on CAF's early years.

CAF docents, past and present, are vital to the story of CAF: Geoffrey Baer, Jane Buckwalter, Tom Carmichael, Kathleen Carpenter, Tom Drebenstedt, Donna Gabanski, Bill Hinchliff, Robert Irving, Henry Kuehn (also a member of the board of trustees), Barbara Lanctot, Diane Lanigan, Joe LaRue, Barry Sears, Ellen Shubart, Jill Tanz and Don Wiberg.

The CAF staff, past and present, were generous in recounting their work for the organization. They include Susan Benjamin, Zurich Esposito, Jill Farley, Barbara Gordon, Bonita Mall, Vicki Matranga, Jennifer Lucente McElroy, Jason Neises, Molly Page, Krisann Rehbein and Hallie Rosen.

People who have served, and still serve, as board of trustees members were important in helping chronicle the evolution of the organization. They include John DiCiurcio, Walt Eckenhoff, Phil Enquist, Jan Grayson, Jeffrey Jahns, Lloyd Morgan, John Pintozzi, John Syvertsen, John Thorpe (who was also a docent and who passed away shortly after our interview), John Tolva and Vic Vickery.

Partner organizations and individuals are crucial to CAF's ability to function at a high level, and many of their representatives were generous in interviews about their work with the organization. They include Bob Agra and Holly Agra, owners of Chicago's First Lady Cruises; Brenna Berman of the City of Chicago,

Bill Donnell of the Monadnock Building, Lori Healey, formerly Mayor Richard M. Daley's chief of staff and later CEO of the Metropolitan Pier and Exposition Authority; Katherine Newhouse and Bev Meland, formerly of the Newhouse Competition; Dominic Pacyga of Columbia College, Charles Shanabruch of St. Xavier University; Elory Rozner; Bill Steers of ArcelorMittal; and Catherine Tinker of Columbia Model and Exhibit Works.

Many architects have given time to CAF over the years, and many of them provided interviews about their experiences. They include Catherine Baker, Joel Berman, Reed Kroloff, Brad Lynch, Sam Marts, Patricia Saldaña Natke, Donna Robertson, Carlo Parente and Lee Weintraub.

Another important category of participant in CAF's success have been educators including Fonda Baldwin of Chicago City Day School; Jill Wine-Banks, an attorney who undertook a leading role at the Chicago Public Schools; and Melissa Barbier and Therese Laslo, formerly of the Chicago Public Schools.

Last but not least are some students who were involved in CAF programs, studied architecture and later worked in local firms and studios. They include Brenda Gamboa, Mario Romero, Fariha Wajid and Michael Wu.

INTRODUCTION

I noticed the four dogs first. Two German shepherds, a golden retriever and a yellow lab. They had led their humans off the busy Chicago sidewalk one August afternoon and into the atrium space of our Railway Exchange Building headquarters. As I crossed paths with the four blind adults—unsure of where they were—I introduced myself, welcomed them to CAF and asked if I could be of any help. They were in town for the large national convention of the Foundation Fighting Blindness and had come inside our building after noticing the smooth terra cotta panels they had felt along the Jackson Boulevard entrance.

As we chatted about the types of experiences they could find at CAF, none of the opportunities were the right fit. A walking tour—designed for the sighted—would have been too difficult. Our main exhibition at the time had only flat panels with text and images. What else could they do here? What else could they 'see'?

I led them into our CitySpace Gallery which had opened a few months earlier. The space included a small exhibition orientating visitors to the city's architecture, a collection of building fragments collected during CAF's early days at Glessner House and our first scale model of downtown.

It was August 2002. I was a young member of CAF's education department, having been on staff for about two years. Despite knowing that the fragile scale model was not to be touched, I took one woman's arm and guided her to the Hancock Tower. As she carefully traced the 3D model with her fingers, I explained how Hancock's trussed tube system provided stability against the wind. She was amazed. "All these years," she said, "I never knew what people meant when they said there were 'X's on the building." Looking back, it was one of the most powerful teaching moments in my 16 years at CAF.

For the past 50 years, this is what CAF has done and continues to do—inspire people of all ages and backgrounds to truly *see* the city.

As an architectural educator and a historian, these moments at CAF of empowering students, educators, docent trainees and the general public with new skills—to see, 'read', then speak about a building for the very first time—are the most memorable. As we inspire Chicagoans to look carefully at the design of a building or a neighborhood, *their* relationship with the built environment changes. Citizens—young and old—who are more informed and engaged in their communities and who understand why design matters, will make better choices for all cities and advocate for higher standards in architecture and urban design.

When thinking about CAF's history, we often refer to "the red book," a 1986 text by Marian Despres on *The First Twenty Years of the Chicago Architecture Foundation*. Despres's leadership on the board of trustees for more than two decades helped bring the organization and docent corps to life. Her descriptions illustrated how CAF has always inspired people to discover why design matters.

This book, *Seeing the City,* builds on her work and celebrates the thousands of docents, volunteers, staff and board members who have dedicated so much of their time, talents, enthusiasm, resources and creativity to CAF. The images and stories from the past 50 years may remind us how our city has changed. But they also show CAF's lasting imprint on the city—empowering people to see Chicago's past, present and future with new eyes.

Jen Masengarb
Director of Interpretation and Research

Loop
Architectura
Walking
Tour

Sta

Tuesdays
Thursdays
Saturdays
10 A.ℳ

Sponsored by
The Chicago Institute of Archit

CHAPTER ONE

BUILDING OF AN IDEA

1966 The Foundation for the Chicago School of Architecture is founded to save the Glessner House (H. H. Richardson, 1887) from destruction. The resolution creating the organization was signed by Carl Condit, Richard Nickel, Herman Pundt, Earl Reed, Wilbert Hasbrouck, James Speyer, Joseph Benson, Clement Sylvestro, George Danforth, Maurice English, Phyllis Lambert, Dirk Lohan, Paul Lurie, Richard Wintergreen, James Schultz, Dan Murphy, Ben Weese, Harry Weese and Irving Berman. 1967 CAF organizes first exhibit, *The Chicago School of Architecture,* curated by Richard Nickel, John Vinci, Wayne Benjamin, Bob Peters and others. CAF holds its first public lecture at Glessner House—Executive Director, L. Morgan Yost presented, "Greene and Greene, Maybeck, Wright and Their Contemporaries." 1968 Carl Condit lectures to 75 people at Glessner House for $.50/person. 1970 CAF has over 100 members, one paid full-time executive director and one half-time staff. Glessner House is designated the City of Chicago's first official landmark and listed on the National Register of Historic Places. 1971 Docent Program graduates the first class of 33 docents and the Docent Council is formed. CAF offers 2 tours, Glessner House and Chicago Loop (from the steps of the Cultural Center), 4 times/week for $1 per person. The year ends by serving 3,000 tour takers. CAF runs a shop and tour center for a short time in the Rookery lobby. 1972 CAF's Auxiliary Board is formed. CAF offers third tour, "The Frank Lloyd Wright Home and Studio in Oak Park." 1973 CAF publishes first tour brochure. First youth education tour, "Put your Arms around a Building." 1974 First Aux Board event, "The Rose Tea," to honor the visit of Mrs. Glessner's granddaughter, Martha Lee Batchelder. CAF has over 1,500 members, staff of 4 and more than 200 docents. William Storrer lectures on "Frank Lloyd Wright and the Energy Crisis" to 200 people. 1975 Auxiliary Board hosts CAF's first gala, Rookery Ball.

JOHN HANCOCK CENTER · CHICAGO, ILLINOIS
ARCHITECTS: SKIDMORE, OWINGS & MERRILL
CONTRACTOR: TISHMAN CONSTRUCTION CO.
DATE: 11/9/67 VIEW: N.E. NEG #152

above: The demolition of Henry Ives Cobb's 1905 Federal Building to make way for the Mies van der Rohe-designed Federal Center. Circa 1965. (Photo: CAF archives)

right: The John Hancock Center under construction. November 9, 1967.
(Photo: Skidmore, Owings & Merrill)

In 1966, the year the Chicago Architecture Foundation (CAF) was created, appreciation of Chicago's architectural legacy was fragmentary. Northwestern University Professor Carl Condit had recently published *The Chicago School of Architecture,* which defined one narrative of Chicago's late 19th century commercial skyscrapers. But urban renewal, the enemy of historic buildings, was being conducted by something cheerfully called the "Land Clearance Commission." The John Hancock Center was going up. Henry Ives Cobb's 1905 Federal Building was coming down.

Those who saw Chicago architecture as a cultural resource were lonely at the time, but they were also tireless, and many of their names are now incised in the history of the organization. First among many was Ben Weese, who tells the story—a founding story—that in 1961 he had been recruited to take the great Finnish architect Alvar Aalto on a tour of Chicago. It didn't go well at first. "It was very difficult because he did not want to look at any buildings–he was not interested in Sullivan or Wright," said Weese, who was almost at a loss when he suggested that they have a look at Glessner House. He told Aalto that it was "a derelict building by [Henry Hobson] Richardson."

1966-1975

When they got there, Aalto was mesmerized. Weese remembered that there were trucks zooming by on 18th Street, but Aalto hardly moved as his eye panned over the soot-covered stone walls. They walked around for an hour, and though Weese knew the importance of the building and of Richardson, this was when he understood with clarity that Glessner House needed to be saved. "It was the bee in the bonnet," Weese said, but in fact it was one of many things that galvanized people who were searching for ways to spread the idea that Chicago architecture mattered and needed to be saved.

Getting the word out about preservation was already urgent, though the call to action was often too faint to hear. In 1957, a small group organized the Chicago Heritage Committee when Frank Lloyd Wright's Robie House in Hyde Park was threatened with destruction. They found a way to save that landmark, but it turned out to be an isolated success. The Loop's Garrick Theater, designed by Adler and Sullivan, went down despite pickets who protested plans to demolish it. A string of other important Loop buildings were blithely razed to make room for larger commercial structures. Still, many people, including architect John Vinci and photographer Richard Nickel, as well as Ben Weese and his brother Harry, were behind the preservation cause when the owners of Glessner House said it was for sale. It was 1963, and the place was hardly on prime commercial real estate. They quickly imagined saving it and making it a center for architectural history.

A FLEDGLING MOVEMENT

The asking price of $70,000 for Glessner House seemed high, but so was the importance of the building in the history of architecture. Its architect, Richardson, stood as an undisputed innovator in developing a characteristically American style, called the Richardsonian Romanesque. Glessner House was recognized as a prime example with its fortress-like strength, flowing interior space and abundant natural light. It had been a clear inspiration for Louis Sullivan. For many other late 19th-century skyscraper designers, Richardson was an iconic figure.

The Weeses and others believed Glessner House could be a home and touchstone for a new organization. Harry Weese, already a nationally-renowned architect, stated an idea in words that seemed quixotic at the time, but now appear visionary: "To create an institution to become the center of architectural history, a staging point for tours, a place to see books and literature, a gallery, a museum for artifacts in the courtyard."

The appeal was heard first by Chicago's small preservation community. Among them was Wilbert (Bill) Hasbrouck, chairman of the preservation committee of the Chicago Chapter of the American Institute of Architects, and Marian Despres, civic leader and wife of the "liberal conscience of Chicago" Alderman Leon Despres. Raising private funds would be a hurdle, but when Harry Weese showed the house to architect Philip Johnson, visiting from New York, Johnson was encouraging. "The most important house in the country to me," Johnson declared in the Chicago *Daily News* after his visit, and he told Harry Weese that he would handle half of the purchase price. He later modified the offer and gave $10,000, but Johnson's enthusiasm and that of others kept the project in the realm of the possible.

opposite top and bottom left: Glessner House for sale. Circa 1966. (Photo: Richard Nickel, CAF Archives)

opposite bottom right: Richard Nickel, early board member of the Chicago School of Architecture Foundation, protests the 1961 planned demolition of Louis Sullivan's Garrick Theater. (Photo: Chicago Sun-Times)

Marian Despres on the courtyard steps of Glessner House in the Spring of 1970. Despres was an early benefactor and served as board of trustees chair for seven years. Spring 1970. (Photo: CAF archives)

Early in 1966—when the house was formally on the market—four other individuals in their 20s joined together to bring some additional force to the effort. Two worked in the office of Mies van der Rohe: architects Richard Wintergreen and James Schultz. The other two were lawyer Paul Lurie and investment banker Wayne Benjamin. As they entered the discussion, they addressed aspects of the house beyond the strictly architectural. For one, they doubted that the asking price was a fair one, and they were right. Based on demolition costs (the preservationist's friend in that period) they convinced the current owners, a research group called the Graphic Arts Technical Foundation, to cut the figure in half. That triggered a new series of pledges of support.

Even as money surfaced to buy the house, some donors doubted that Weese's vision was plausible. When the firm of Perkins + Will gave $5,000 toward the purchase, the donation came with Larry Perkins's dreary prediction: "My partners and I do not believe that Glessner House can be restored to a living, breathing institution in the foreseeable future." Other money came not because the project was promising, but because they felt something had to be done to support historic buildings. The Graham Foundation's director, John Entenza, gave $5,000 from that organization. Phyllis Lambert, Seagram's heiress and an Illinois Institute of Technology (IIT)-trained architect; Leon and Marian Despres; C.F. Murphy and Co.; and Skidmore, Owings and Merrill (SOM) all promised significant amounts without going on record that it looked like money down the drain.

A HOUSE "TO WORK FOR A LIVING"

As funds toward purchasing Glessner House began to be pledged, it was time to bring an official organization into existence. On April 16, 1966, the founders assembled to sign a document which created the Foundation For the Chicago School of Architecture. (That name would be changed within a few months to the Chicago School of Architecture Foundation, and by 1977 to the Chicago Architecture Foundation.) Signing the resolution were the Weeses, Despres, Nickel (who promised an inaugural exhibit of salvage ornament), Benjamin, Hasbrouck, Lambert, Lohan, Lurie, Schultz, Joseph Benson, Irving Berman, George Danforth, Maurice English, Dan Murphy, Herman Pundt, Earl Reed, Jim Speyer and Clement Sylvestro.

On December 14, 1966, the organization closed on its purchase of Glessner House, which was being heated (just barely) with electric space heaters. For another year at least, meetings of the board met at Glessner House when temperatures permitted and at Harry Weese's office on the North Side when they did not. At an April 1967 meeting of the CSAF (held at the Weese office), current business involved the encouraging news that the Illinois Arts Council was showing an interest in funding the organization. An accessions committee announced plans to acquire furnishings for the house and also salvaged ornament from historic buildings that were continuing to go down at an alarming rate.

Also at that meeting, the program committee reported that they had a list of the activities that appeared suitable for the organization moving forward. These included tours, both of Glessner House and of late 19th-century Chicago School buildings in the Loop, while exhibits and lectures could be conducted

top: An early board of trustees meeting in Glessner House library. At the desk (left to right): Richard Wintergreen and Paul Lurie; First row: Irving Berman, Wayne Benjamin, unknown; Second row: unknown, Marian Despres, Dan Brenner, Dirk Lohan; Third row: unknown, Carl Condit, Ben Weese, unknown. August 1966. (Photo: Richard Nickel, Glessner House archives)

bottom: President Richard Wintergreen removes the "For Sale" sign shortly after Glessner House was purchased in 1966. (Photo: Richard Nickel, CAF Archives)

1966–1975

at the House. Someone mentioned that an oral history project connected to Chicago architecture might be organized. The program committee also hoped that other organizations could take up residence at Glessner House. The organization could consider a bookstore, a "publishing center" and a library for documents and historical drawings.

While these plans generated enthusiasm, there were also practical considerations, such as overnight security for Glessner House as the neighborhood dealt with demolitions, abandonment and crime. This was achieved that year when Charles Jackson, an older gentleman from the neighborhood, moved in. Jackson was a picturesque figure who claimed to be 90 years old and probably was. His apartment, with a door just inside the main entry, often filled the rest of the house with the fragrance of onions, cabbage and cigar smoke. He also owned a gun and displayed it whenever possible, on the theory that word would get around that breaking in was a bad idea.

In early 1967, the board chose L. Morgan Yost, a semi-retired architect, to take the position of executive director. As a noted residential architect, Yost was well-suited to oversee the project of replacing a "dead leviathan" of a furnace with seven zoned units. Properly heated, Glessner House could finally accommodate Yost, his skeletal staff of one administrative assistant, historian Susan Synikin (later Benjamin), and an active corps of volunteers.

People were well aware of what Ben Weese had said a few months before: "This is a landmark that will have to work for a living." And it was. In September 1967, the minutes of that month's board meeting indicated that the Chicago office of the Historical American Building Survey (HABS), a federal project to document significant architecture, was quartered in the dining room. The Lake Michigan Regional Planning occupied two bedrooms upstairs. Eventually several preservation and architecture-based organizations provided rental income by moving their headquarters into the house, including the Chicago Chapter of the American Institute of Architects, the Landmarks Preservation Council of Illinois, *Inland Architect,* the Illinois State Historic Survey and the Midwest Office of the National Trust for Historic Preservation.

With reliable heat and a few rent-paying tenants, the founders got started with exhibitions and programs. In the fall of 1967, Richard Nickel, John Vinci, Wayne Benjamin and Bob Peters, among others, curated the first exhibition. "The Chicago School of Architecture" was held in conjunction with an early 1968 lecture by Carl Condit, who spoke on his pioneering work in defining the Chicago School. Bill Hasbrouck spoke on the preservation movement then dawning in Chicago not only at Glessner, but in Nickel's efforts at Sullivan's Stock Exchange Building, and Harry Weese and Associates' work in saving the Auditorium Building.

"With the growing attendance and interest in these lectures, we discussed the possibility of opening the second floor of the carriage house for larger lecture space" (as documented in the minutes of April 5, 1968). But Yost told his enthusiastic board to slow down. "Let's pay the bills we have first. Also—he is anxious to have a period of cleaning up [as] alteration work does make much dust and dirt."

opposite: In 1966, preservationist and photographer, Richard Nickel captures a series of photos showing President Richard Wintergreen removing the Graphic Arts Technical Foundation sign from Glessner House. (Photos: Richard Nickel, CAF Archives)

1966-1975

"To create an institution to become the center of architectural history, a staging point for tours, a place to see books and literature, a gallery, a museum for artifacts in the courtyard."

HARRY WEESE, ARCHITECT
AND BOARD OF TRUSTEES PRESIDENT, 1967

The What and Why of Louis Sullivan's Architecture, a 1968 exhibition was held at Glessner House, included building fragments salvaged by Richard Nickel and John Vinci. (Photo: CAF Archives)

above right: McCormick Place on the Lake: Innovations in Architecture, a 1971 exhibition at Glessner House, was curated by Robert Peters.

opposite: The demolition of the Keith mansion's north wall, forming Glessner House's courtyard, was halted at the last minute by board of trustees member Ben Weese one morning in 1968.
(Photo: Richard Nickel, CAF Archives)

REASSEMBLING THE PAST

Proper restoration plans—with board members like Hasbrouck, John Vinci and Bob Peters of SOM all contributing—could only be undertaken slowly and as resources were found. Yet not every project was discretionary. A nasty surprise arrived one morning in 1968 when wreckers began to demolish the once-splendid Keith mansion next door. As the Keiths's north wall constituted the south wall of the Glessners's courtyard—the courtyard being a key design element—someone phoned Ben Weese who raced down to 18th Street. He convinced the wreckers to hold off while he called the house's owner, R.R. Donnelley and Company. Donnelley agreed to delay long enough for the organization to find a way to save the wall. This preservation triumph cost the organization about $11,000, which it scrambled to raise.

Restoration went ahead haltingly, but with promising successes. For example, director Yost traveled east to meet the grandchildren of Frances and John J. Glessner, who had been a founder of International Harvester. John Glessner Lee lived in Connecticut, and Martha Lee Batchelder was summering at The Rocks, the New Hampshire estate where the Glessners had spent their summers for a half century. The grandchildren opened family archives to Yost, including Richardson drawings and showed him heirlooms of furniture and decorative arts. The Glessners and the organization quickly became allies, and the family promised the first of many shipments of furnishings that had been removed from the house when John J. Glessner died in 1936.

Things went slowly but surely at Glessner House. In 1973, Marian and Leon Despres agreed to underwrite the restoration of what had been the most important room in the house, the library. It became the Alfred Alschuler Memorial Library, named for the distinguished architect and Marian's father. Richardson intended for the Glessner library to be the most personal reflection of the family who lived in the house, and thus it had a prominent place in the corner of the first floor. The room had been a masterpiece of the Arts and Crafts style and was recreated with the original desk (which had been left behind), the brass fireplace surround (which was found in a Glessner family barn) and other period objects. The "Bird and Vine" pattern in the draperies—known from photos—was reproduced on the looms of Scalamandré in England. They were the only firm that could properly weave in the manner of the original William Morris fabric.

The library was slowly coming into shape when members of the organization did something else that they did very well and often—host a reception. This time it was for Mrs. Batchelder: a "Rose Tea," as it was called, featuring decor and refreshments as Mrs. Glessner had at least once detailed in her journal. The granddaughter was dazzled by this, later sending additional furniture and decorative arts to the organization for the library and other rooms as they were being filled out.

As the Glessner House project moved forward, board of trustee members learned about the pleasures of preservation but also became attuned to its risks. For example, among the largely volunteer architects involved was a former associate of Mies van der Rohe who proposed to reconfigure a string of downstairs rooms to create a series of *interpenetrating* spaces, as it could be charitably described. Miesians cited a direct evolution from Richardson's space planning to the International style, but the stark lines and spare ornament proposed were too much for many board members to take. The idea of "adaptive reuse" was moderated in favor of "accurate restoration" at Glessner, as Marian Despres shared in her 20-year history of CAF written in 1986.

THE ORGANIZATION'S VOLUNTARY SPIRIT

The volunteer culture of the Chicago Architecture Foundation was embodied in many people who are remembered dearly in the annals of the early organization. Among them was Jeanette Fields, not fully a volunteer as she was part-time staff and paid administrator. Fields shared a passion for the organization's mission as she untiringly gave tours of Glessner House and performed countless other duties. She lived in a Frank Lloyd Wright-designed house in Oak Park and understood Glessner's significance. She often brought cut flowers from her garden for the house-museum's living room table. Fields was also an experienced public relations operative, and no one was as effective at getting coverage in the press at the time.

Fields's enthusiasm was contagious. Among the people she brought in were John Thorpe and Linda Legner; Thorpe was a young architect at SOM at the time, Legner had a position in marketing. The two first ventured to Glessner House one Saturday morning where Fields gave them her hour-long tour of the house. When she was finished she asked if they might like to give the tour themselves some weekends. They said yes and were recruited on the spot to be among CAF's first docents. Another was Bob Irving, a recent arrival in Chicago to teach humanities

opposite top: Glessner House receiving a new roof in 1974. (Photo: CAF Archives)

opposite bottom: Mrs. Alfred Alschuler (seated), wife of the late Chicago architect, is surrounded by her family members and daughter Marian Alschuler Despres in Glessner House library. The family funded the room's faithful restoration in 1973–1974. (Photo: Glessner House Archives)

above: A "Rose Tea" is held in Glessner House courtyard in 1974 to celebrate the visit of Martha Lee Batchelder, granddaughter of the Glessners, visiting Chicago from New Hampshire. (Photo: CAF Archives)

at IIT. When he saw a light on in Glessner he knocked on the door, took Fields's tour and was invited to join the first "docent class" in 1971.

These newcomers could be excused for not knowing what a docent was at the time. It was a little-known term in Chicago when Marian Despres envisioned a corps of volunteer guides based on a program used at Gamble House in Pasadena, California, the house-museum designed by Greene and Greene in the Craftsman style. Gamble House docents, she had learned, were well-trained and known for giving fascinating tours. This gave her the vision to do something similar for Glessner House.

The volunteer idea at Glessner House was a necessity, of course, as there was no money to organize tours on any other basis. But the docents' enthusiasm and ultimately their independence took on a life of its own, and these qualities quickly became the organization's greatest strength. The first docent course, taught by architectural historians Carl Condit and Paul Sprague was conducted for two hours each Saturday morning for seven weeks. The class included 36 prospective docents. Walking and bus tours, along with lectures on topics such as "What is Architecture?" and "Richardson, Sullivan and Wright" were intended to give the docent trainees a deep understanding of the subject matter. As the course proceeded, homework was evaluated and examinations were given by a committee of existing volunteers, staff and board members. This was the beginning of a unique model of peer-to-peer training, now a permanent hallmark of docent education at CAF.

On June 12, 1971, 33 docents graduated in a ceremony that was staged on the north steps of the Chicago Public Library (now the Cultural Center), and covered by the press and television. As board of trustees chair, Despres officially welcomed the new docents to the volunteer ranks of the organization. Regular tours of Glessner House and historic Loop skyscrapers began right away.

Demand for tours was evident from the beginning; a remarkable 3,000 people took tours by the end of the year. In 1972, the second docent class graduated 34, with seven dropping out as the course proved too rigorous. The docent idea was looking like a great success by the following summer when several docents thought up and organized a new set of neighborhood tours. John Thorpe wrote and gave Oak Park tours that visited a number of Frank Lloyd Wright-designed houses, including the rooming house that would later be restored as the Wright Home and Studio. Thorpe warned visitors not to ask the rooming house owner about Wright's famous indiscretions lest they be kicked out and not invited back. Bob Irving wrote and gave a North Michigan Avenue tour. Devereux (Dev) Bowly, a lawyer and ardent preservationist, created a Hyde Park tour. In time, volunteers would write and deliver 150 different tours that were as specialized and as fascinating as the personal interests of the docents giving them.

PRAIRIE AVENUE HISTORIC DISTRICT

From its founding, CAF's ideas involved the full scope of architecture. So while the organization was selecting fabric for draperies, it was also imagining a historic landmark district around Glessner House. Led by Leon Despres, the City Council passed a historic preservation ordinance in February 1969. The house was the first

above: Marian Despres (board of trustees chair) and Jeanette Fields (executive director) at a Glessner House reception. Circa 1975. (Photo: CAF Archives)

opposite top left: The button that docent Henry Kuehn proudly received upon his graduation from the docent training program. (Courtesy: Henry Kuehn)

oppposite top right: The massive stone arch of the servant's entrance, on the north side of Glessner House, inspired the first logo for the organization. (Photo: Glessner House Archives)

opposite bottom: Board of trustees chair Marian Despres introduces members of the first docent class on the steps of the Chicago Public Library (now the Chicago Cultural Center) at their graduation in 1971. (Photo: CAF Archives)

building to be considered for designation as a Chicago landmark, and was included in the first group of landmarks designated in October 1970. While individual houses could be designated as landmarks, the ordinance included the possibility of neighborhoods as well. This was certainly written with Prairie Avenue in mind. Marian Despres believed, as she later wrote, that Glessner House could not flourish as an "isolated architectural element." Rather it existed as "part of a larger urban environment."

Just how large this environment should be was a question, of course. As early as 1967, Phyllis Lambert, then in the office of Mies van der Rohe, endeavored to define what a historic district might look like. Lambert wrote in a report that the Prairie Avenue area was layered with history reaching back to the 1812 Battle of Fort Dearborn, which took place just a few steps away, and was later the first home of Chicago's great industrial families. Lambert also believed that the district should influence "a general plan of the northern sector of the South Side," a patchwork of neighborhoods in decline. She noted that a stately past, as well as its proximity to the Loop, could make the historic district an effective counterweight to abandonment and neglect.

Creating a proper historic district would take time, but the effort was taken up by Chicago School of Architecture Foundation (CSAF) board member Ruth Moore Garbe, a former *Chicago Sun-Times* reporter. Then in 1972, Mayor Richard J. Daley created a Prairie Avenue Historic District Committee, led jointly by the city and CSAF, (and co-chaired by Garbe) to determine how to proceed. A concrete sign of the city's resolve came in 1974 when it embarked on the acquisition and restoration of the Henry B. Clarke House. It was the city's oldest surviving building, from 1836, and it would be a million-dollar-plus project to move it from

4526 South Wabash Avenue to a site on Indiana Avenue, adjacent to the back of Glessner House. The National Society of the Colonial Dames of America in the State of Illinois agreed to furnish it, while the CSAF agreed to manage tours. By 1975, an Ann Arbor landscape firm called Preservation Urban Design detailed the streetscapes of Prairie Avenue and environs with cobblestones and gas lamps.

Scores of details, from the architectural to the political, were necessary before the vision begun in 1967 was realized. There were glitches; architects were delayed when they could not find limestone sidewalk slabs that were the same size as those used when the neighborhood was Chicago's most elite residential area. Finally in 1978, the district was opened with a three-day celebration sponsored by Marshall Field and Co. (Marshall Field was a Prairie Avenue resident.) The City Council made the Prairie Avenue Historic District an official landmark the next year.

The district is smaller than Phyllis Lambert had originally proposed; it includes the five surviving mansions on the 1800 and 1900 blocks of South Prairie Avenue, the site of the Battle of Fort Dearborn, and a grouping of three row houses on the 200 block of East Cullerton Street. The planners at one point proposed that they might add a balloon frame building to the cluster of houses by Glessner, also a house of later vintage—these to illustrate the development of architecture over a relatively short period of time. While those plans were not realized, the district was called an "outdoor museum of urban change." It was an apt description, especially as an offshoot of the organization which had been founded thirteen years prior in order to preserve the built fabric of Chicago even as it changed.

top left: An early board of trustees and membership meeting of the Chicago School of Architecture Foundation in Glessner House courtyard. Circa 1973. (Photo: Glessner House Archives)

top right: Docents lead walking tours of the newly-formed Prairie Avenue Historic District and Glessner House on the right. Circa 1978. (Photo: CAF Archives)

How the Chicago Architecture Foundation trains docents

Apply *for the CAF docent education program*

Interview *with CAF docents and staff*

Help *train and welcome new docents*

Develop *new tours, train for new tours, sit on committees*

Lead *tours for enthusiastic visitors*

Certify *for the tour with a CAF docent certifier*

Join **the CAF docent program**

Learn **the "Fundamentals of Chicago Architecture"** *(5 full-day sessions)*

Train **for two of CAF's tours** *(9 full-day sessions) with readings, lectures, explorations of the city, best practices, hands-on activities, homework*

Practice, practice, practice **with a CAF docent sponsor**

Receive **feedback on homework from a CAF docent reader**

CHAPTER TWO

CREATING
AN IMPASSIONED
AUDIENCE

1976 Illinois' theme for the national Bicentennial celebration is "Illinois Architecture: Revolution on the Prairie," and the Illinois Arts Council gives CAF the contract to manage a downtown center for exhibits, lectures and meetings. The term "ArchiCenter" is coined for the center and opens in the Loop at 111 South Dearborn. Approximately 5,000 visitors a month come to the ArchiCenter that year. First "Highlights by Bus" tour. 1977 The Board drops "School" from its title and the organization is renamed "The Chicago Architecture Foundation." 1978 CAF has over 1,600 members. ArchiCenter moves to the Straus Building at 310 South Michigan. 1979 The first L tour runs in July. 1980 Mission statement: "The purpose of the Chicago Architecture Foundation is to increase the level of awareness, understanding and appreciation of Chicago's culture manifested in its past, present and future environment." 1981 CAF moves the ArchiCenter to the Monadnock Building. 1982 CAF reaches 2,330 members. Newhouse Architecture Competition for high school students begins under the leadership of Senator Richard Newhouse, SOM and CPS. 1983 CAF launches first river tour. 1984 CAF has 250 active docents. 1985 CAF offers over 40 tours of Chicago and suburbs. 1990 Mission statement: "The mission of the Chicago Architecture Foundation is to advance public interest and education in the areas of architecture and urban design." Vincent Scully lectures at CAF.

The organization was still called the Chicago School of Architecture Foundation (CSAF) when its center of gravity shifted north in 1976. That year, the ArchiCenter, a tour center and exhibit space, opened in the Loop. It seemed like an inevitable move as the downtown walking tours of Chicago skyscrapers had become popular, and the growing docent corps was developing new tours for other parts of the city. In fact, the ArchiCenter was not part of any long-term planning by the organization at the time. It was conceived when the Illinois Arts Council was seeking ways to participate in the American Bicentennial.

To solicit ideas, Council chair Bruce Sagan called a meeting of arts and cultural organizations statewide, and attendee Jeanette Fields had a ready answer: promote architecture, for which Chicago was famous throughout the world. Sagan was convinced. The state chose "Illinois Architecture: Revolution on the Prairie" as a Bicentennial theme, and CSAF opened the ArchiCenter at Dearborn and Monroe Streets as part of this celebration.

The first ArchiCenter, located on the empty second floor of the now-demolished Amalgamated Bank Building, might have seemed shopworn and even shabby, but its location was absolutely prime real estate for exploring the city's architecture. It was on Monroe Street across from the Inland Steel Building which was sleek and undeniably innovative, even at 18 years old. The Marquette Building, a big-shouldered late 19th century skyscraper, was a few steps down Dearborn Street. The sloping profile of the new First National Bank (now Chase Tower) was kitty-corner Architecture was everywhere, and the organization, with a small staff and impassioned docents, was as eager as ever to explain it.

The first ArchiCenter, located across Monroe Street from the Inland Steel Building on Dearborn Street, opened in 1976 as part of the Illinois celebration of the American Bicentennial.

The ArchiCenter sold tickets for tours and explained architecture in other ways. A permanent gallery used large photos to dramatize Chicago's role as the birthplace of skyscrapers and the Chicago School. John Vinci designed an exhibit of poster-size photographs of architectural landmarks that were familiar to Chicagoans in many ways except for perhaps their significance. Actually the first scene that visitors saw when they came up the escalator was not a building at all, but Chicago's charred remains in 1871, suggesting that Chicago rose stronger from the ashes after the Great Fire.

Chicago embraced the ArchiCenter as it stoked civic pride. "The city's most splendorous treasure is its architecture," wrote architecture critic Paul Gapp in an article about the new center. In April 1976, dedication ceremonies brought out dignitaries and included Nancy Hanks, chairman of the National Endowment for the Arts. As they lauded the new facility, they pushed the relatively new idea that important old buildings could, and must, be saved. The ArchiCenter would "shape an informed and interested public," wrote the *Tribune* in its editorial pages. "But unless the will to preserve landmarks is implemented... many more notable Chicago buildings will go the way of the Garrick Theatre."

The preservation argument was an emotional one at that time, not strongly economic as it would become. The Bicentennial had done its job—it made history one ingredient of America's strength. Indeed, the economic case for preservation was still a hard one as expensive successes, like Glessner and Clarke houses—the latter restored by Bill Hasbrouck—could only demonstrate. But as people flowed into the ArchiCenter for "brown bag" lectures, to visit new exhibits, take short tours of the Loop designed for the lunch crowd, and attend after-work screenings of movies about architecture, it was almost instantly clear that there was support for historic buildings and for the organization as well.

While "architecture exhibits" were not common fare in many museums at the time, the ArchiCenter hosted and mounted new ones constantly. "Women in American Architecture," organized by the Smithsonian, made the point that women had made an impact despite a long and ongoing fight against discrimination in the profession. Paul Gapp admired the exhibit in print, especially the inclusion of Chicagoans such as Skidmore Owings & Merrill's Natalie de Blois, a key participant in mid-century designs like Chicago's Equitable and New York's Union Carbide buildings, for which she rarely got ample credit. She was "a classic victim of chauvinism," Gapp wrote. Another early exhibit was "Recycled Chicago," with photographs of vintage buildings repurposed for modern use, ranging from masterpieces like the Auditorium, to workhorses like Sauer's Restaurant.

By summer 1976, the ArchiCenter was receiving 5,000 visitors a month, a triumph by any standard, but especially for an organization that began in a derelict house on a neglected street just ten years earlier. "It was a heady time," said Vicki Matranga who managed the ArchiCenter. "We really believed we were at the beginning of something, and that included the preservation movement." Nevertheless, by the end of the year there was fear for the ArchiCenter's survival. Money that was coming from the state was going to expire with the Bicentennial, and there was no concrete plan to keep it open.

So the organization did what it had done before: it sent out an urgent appeal for money. About $16,000 was quickly secured from private sources to pay the

top left: During the preservation battles of the 1960s and 1970s, CAF shed light on Loop structures lost to the wrecking ball. Circa 1977. (Photo: CAF Archives)

top right: Architect John Vinci (left) helped to curate several exhibitions at CAF in the late 1960s and 1970s, including one highlighting his work with Richard Nickel in preserving the Auditorium Theater. (Photo: CAF Archives)

middle: A 1978 exhibition, *Women in American Architecture,* highlighted the ground-breaking work of historic and contemporary architects, including Marion Mahoney Griffin and Natalie de Blois. (Photo: CAF Archives)

bottom: Long-time board of trustees chair Marian Despres and her husband, Alderman Leon Despres, in the courtyard of the Glessner House. Circa 1976. (Photo: CAF Archives)

ArchiCenter rent for another year, Marian Despres, then chair, explained that the 1977 operating budget of $120,000 was still unaccounted for. They could depend on $55,000 in tour fees and "gift counter" revenue, but for the rest they needed private donations, which amounted—she wryly stated—to the salaries of four city workers. Publicity and steady fund-raising worked, and the organization announced that its Loop outpost would survive another year.

THE DOCENT CORPS

A clear sign of Chicago architecture's new prestige could be found in the growing numbers of CAF docents. By 1976, some 200 people had taken the training course. It was a selective group, and not everyone who applied was accepted, but those who served gave tours regularly. Many of these volunteers proposed and wrote new tours as appropriate to CAF's mission and were marketable to the public. Some joined the docent council—the governing body of the docent corps—which remains today. Others served as sponsors and certifiers for new trainees in CAF's unique peer-to-peer learning. It was serious work and, even if unpaid, it attracted serious people.

There was docent Diane Lanigan (class of 1972) whose enthusiasm was illustrative if not typical. (In 2016 she was the longest-serving docent still actively giving tours.) Lanigan had grown up in Kansas and attended Kansas State where she worked on the school paper and once wrote about Frank Lloyd Wright's visit to the campus. "I was impressed by how opinionated he was," she said, "but so surprised at how soft-spoken." She remained attuned to architecture, and by the time she was living in Arlington Heights and her children were in school, she was accepted to CAF's docent education program. She loved giving tours, initially of Glessner House and the Loop and later Oak Park and a popular tour of Graceland Cemetery. Lanigan absolutely provided what CAF needed in docents, which was the ability to personalize her tours. One of her visitors once told her: "I felt like you knew all of these historic architects, like they were your friends." It was the highest praise she could ever want.

There was docent Bill Hinchcliff (class of 1976), a Chicagoan who was teaching high school at the time when he began docent training. Hinchcliff had gone to Yale and had taken Vincent Scully's American architecture course while there. "What hooked me on architecture was Scully's admiration for Frank Lloyd Wright," he said later. Wright's architecture was tied to many elements of the environment, and that clued Hinchcliff into what was fascinating about the Loop tour to him. He explained what influenced Chicago skyscrapers: real estate, economics and technology—not to mention beauty. "The story was so clear. We just had to tell people to look up." It became the call to action at CAF for years to come: "Look up!"

Along with Vicki Matranga, Hinchcliff helped organize a bus tour, a three-hour jaunt with stops all over the city. This tour gave docents the chance to talk about the historical connections among Glessner House and other late 19th century icons around the city. It also drew out-of-towners who, as tourists, had more time to see the "real smorgasbord" of architecture, as Hinchcliff liked to put it. By 1979 he was also giving the "Elevated Chicago" tour which chartered its own CTA train

top: CAF's Graceland Cemetery tour docents gather for a holiday celebration. (left to right) Front row: Bob Cook and Carol Cosimano; Back row: Karen Dimond, Norma Green, Betty McAvoy, Diane Laningan, Barb Lanctot, Mary Alice Malloy, Kathryn Neary, Jeff Nichols and Henry Kuehn. Circa 1982. (Courtesy Henry Kuehn)

bottom: Henry Kuehn's 1974 welcome letter with more information about the seven-week docent training program. "Bring a notebook and your lunch," it said, and purchase a copy of the required text, Carl Condit's the Chicago School of Architecture. (Courtesy Henry Kuehn)

and drew attention to the architecture that flanked many of the city's L train lines. This typified many of the special tours in the growing CAF tour catalogue. It found a small following (it was five hours long) but a passionate one, and was given once a year for more than a decade.

Then there was Henry Kuehn, a senior executive at a pharmaceutical company. In 1974 Kuehn was in mid-career and ready for a new personal challenge. He had studied engineering at Yale and as a diversion from that he, like Hinchcliff, took Vincent Scully's course. Scully's ideas of organic architecture and modernism stayed with Kuehn, especially when he moved to Chicago. When Marian Despres interviewed him, as she interviewed all prospective docents at the time, he made it obvious that he understood Glessner House beyond its furniture and finishes. "I understood how the interior courtyard of Glessner House was unique," Kuehn said. "It showed how architects could break away from the box." This idea of "breaking the box" became an overarching theme of many CAF tours. It could also describe the ambitions of the Chicago Architecture Foundation, as it was renamed in 1977, to grow.

A NEW HOME FOR THE ARCHICENTER

The preservation movement, while moving forward, was hardly blocking the tide of demolitions that were rife in the 1970s. But there were small victories, especially with preservation projects in historic Loop skyscrapers. Federal tax credits later helped make some of these projects feasible, such as the Fisher and Marquette buildings in the Loop, but so did the education of the public, in which CAF played such an important role. In 1979, when Bill Donnell led an investment group to buy the Monadnock Building, it became a blend of idealism and practicality. The project inspired him to make the 1891–1893 Burnham and Root / Holabird and Roche structure a "model for preservation nationwide," as the National Trust stated in citing the project with an honor award in 1987.

But neither the Monadnock's floor plan nor the careful restoration appealed to the mega-tenants sought by most Loop developers at the time. Narrow office sizes in the building dictated a more modest list of potential renters, and in 1981 that included the Chicago Architecture Foundation. After leaving the Amalgamated Bank, which was being razed, the ArchiCenter had occupied the second floor of the Straus Building at 310 South Michigan Avenue for three years. In the Monadnock Building, it would get a storefront on the first floor, plus a gallery, lecture hall and some office space on the second floor. With an internal stairway connecting them, the ArchiCenter became a tour center / bookstore/ event venue in a timeless architectural monument.

The new home also inspired an exhibit and lecture schedule that was busier than ever. A small sampling of topics handled in the years that followed included *Hedrich-Blessing: Recent Architectural Photography* in 1983; *Idealism in Industry: Chicago and the Industrial Park* in 1984; *Architectural Ornamentation in Chicago* in 1985; *Tall Buildings in America* in 1986; *Beverly Hills/Morgan Park: Design for Living* in 1986; *Silent Sentinels* on cemetery art and architecture in 1988; *Celebrating Chicago's Religious Architecture* in 1989; and *On the Waterfront: Site-Sensitive Building by the Chicago River* in 1990.

Dear Trainee: We are happy to inform you that you have been accepted in our 1974 Docent training program. We hope that on April 27th you will be a full fledged 'docent'!

JEANETTE FIELDS, EXECUTIVE DIRECTOR,
CHICAGO SCHOOL OF ARCHITECTURE
FOUNDATION TO FUTURE DOCENT HENRY KUEHN
FEBRUARY 20, 1974

top left: The ArchiCenter shop in the Monadnock Building included an expanded collection of books, posters and gifts. Circa 1991. (Photo: CAF Archives)

top right: The ArchiCenter, located on the first and second floors of the Monadnock Building at Dearborn and Van Buren streets, also included an exhibition space. Circa 1991. (Photo: CAF Archives)

right: Regular weekly lectures from architects, historians and authors were given in the late 1980s and early 1990s in the Monadnock Building headquarters. Circa 1991. (Photo: CAF Archives)

FINANCIAL TURNAROUND AND THE RIVER TOUR

The Monadnock move represented visible growth, but there was other movement at CAF less apparent to the public; a gradual shoring up of finances that had been very fragile for several years. The turnaround began ostensibly in 1983 when Robert Hutchins, an architect and Presbyterian minister, was made president of the board of trustees and brought new business controls to the organization. For several years deficits were serious. In the early 1980s, CAF's modest endowment was drawn down, leaving almost nothing to pay for alarming (though predictable) demands of maintaining Glessner House.

Among new board members during this retrenchment was docent Henry Kuehn (class of 1974). Kuehn joined with other board members to guarantee a loan in order to keep the organization's head above fiscal water. Around the same time, a long-range planning committee was established. For survival CAF had to build on the activities that had generated revenue in the past. The organization's membership had reached a respectable 2,500, even in the straits of the financial crisis. Another problem—or opportunity—was the bookstore, which lost many of its regular suppliers when the previous administration had fallen behind on bills. Bonita Mall, the new ArchiCenter manager who would eventually become vice president of tours, exhibitions and education, set that operation on course to generate $20,000 a month within a year.

The most important element of the past and of the future, naturally, was tours, and not just the regular Loop and Glessner House offerings. Considering the knowledge and enthusiasm of docents, a deep tour catalog as varied as Chicago architecture itself quickly developed. They invented bicycle tours of suburbs such as Kenilworth and Riverside. They created cemetery tours—specifically Graceland Cemetery, which became a best-seller. Other tours added to the catalog were a tour of the Pullman neighborhood, a public sculpture tour and, around the time the State of Illinois (now Thompson) Center opened in 1985, a postmodernism tour.

Expansion along these lines was enhanced by the newly visible tour center in the Monadnock Building. "Being downtown made life so much easier for everyone giving the tours," said docent Bob Irving (class of 1971), who in the early 1980s

top left: CAF docents, trustees and architectural enthusiasts await the start of an evening panel discussion at the Monadnock Building. Circa 1989. (Photo: CAF Archives)

top right: CAF evening programs often brought together well-known architects and historians for discussions on new projects. Left to right: Thomas Beeby, Dirk Lohan, Franz Schulze, moderator and Trustee Thomas Samuels, Robert A.M. Stern, Bruce Graham and Bill Brubaker. Circa 1989. (Photo: CAF Archives)

wrote and guided a tour that he called the "Riverwalk." It skirted the Chicago River and looked at old warehouses, new skyscrapers, and historic bridges. A few years later, docent Tom Drebenstedt (class of 1986) expanded on Irving's tour by walking the riverfront to see new postmodern structures such as Kohn Pedersen Fox's 333 West Wacker. These tours were fun for docents and visitors alike because they featured new architecture going up along Wacker Drive, but they also highlighted something else—an "elephant in the room," which was the Chicago River. With high pollution levels, it was not particularly appealing at the time, but it was also ready for a renaissance in which CAF was well suited to participate.

Others had the river in view as well. Friends of the River was formed in 1979 with the goal of promoting the historic waterway as a positive resource. A National Heritage Corridor, including the Chicago River, was being presented to Congress for historic designation. Moreover, some new buildings along the river were no longer designed to turn their backs to the river as many had in the past. These architects of late 20th century buildings began to see the water as an amenity instead of a misfortune. Still, it was a surprise to Bob Irving in 1983 when the organizers of NeoCon, the annual international design convention held at the Merchandise Mart, asked CAF to consider guiding a private boat tour for attendees to look at Chicago from an unusual perspective.

That Chicago architecture looked great from the Chicago River was not a surprise, but it was an epiphany. The NeoCon cruise—with a design-oriented audience—

A docent leads a walking tour near architect Bertrand Goldberg's Marina City, completed ten years prior. May 1974. (Photo: CAF Archives)

top right: Tours expanded beyond Glessner House, Prairie Avenue and the Loop by the late 1970s. Docents developed new neighborhood tours, such as this one in Pullman. Circa 1978. (Photo: CAF Archives)

above: Broadening beyond the late 19th century skyscrapers, docents wrote and gave tours of new buildings, such as Harry Weese's 1968 Seventeenth Church of Christ, Scientist. Circa 1974. (Photo: CAF Archives)

bottom right: Docents wrote new tours in the late 1970s and early 1980s that explored modernist icons, including Ludwig Mies van der Rohe's 1965–1975 Federal Center. Circa 1983. (Photo: CAF Archives)

was a success, and almost immediately Irving took it upon himself to conceive a CAF river tour for the general public. It took some time to find the right boat and the right mooring, but the potential was obvious. Countless views from the boat provided the richest sampling of historic and contemporary milestones—from the site of old Fort Dearborn (near the Michigan Avenue Bridge) to Marina City to the Sears Tower (now Willis Tower) and beyond. It was also a relaxed setting for the tour takers, with docents able to concentrate more on the stories that enriched their tours and less on moving their guests down a sidewalk.

The boat tour would go on to become a great success as time passed, not just for CAF but for Chicago tourism in general. Not to say that there weren't problems along the way. There were low bridges on the north and south branches that might fail to cooperate; a bus once had to come to the rescue. Moreover, the river was less than fully presentable at every turn. For each splendid view there were also reminders of Bubbly Creek's pollution. For each historic bridge there was also urban wildlife racing along the banks. Bob Irving's solution was to repeat the slogan that many docents used. "Look up! Look Up!"

Many followed Irving's advice. And things were looking up, due in part to the success of the boat tour. Both Chicagoans and out-of-towners began to see the river for its history, its vitality, and its growing beauty. Within a few years the river cruise was a blockbuster, thanks to eager docents who passionately shared this new vantage point on architecture with visitors—and they were just getting started. It became an example of CAF teaching Chicagoans to truly see and appreciate their river. The river enjoyed great improvements and even became an asset. CAF's role in the waterway's transformation demonstrated the impact that a dynamic cultural institution could have on the life of the city.

top left: Docent Bill Hinchcliff (left) developed CAF's first bus tour, and docent Bob Irving (right) created the first riverwalk and architectural boat tour. Circa 1979. (Photo: CAF Archives)

top right: Tour takers saw Bertrand Goldberg's innovative new "city within a city" towers of Marina City. Circa 1974. (Photo: CAF Archives)

Growth of the Chicago Architecture Foundation

1,000,000
hours donated by thousands of volunteers (the equivalent of more than 110 years)

250,000
students served

10,000,000
people reached through all CAF experiences

CAF tour guests have walked the equivalent of 80 trips around the world—or enough to walk every inch of every street in Chicago 500 times!

CHAPTER THREE

LEARNING THROUGH ARCHITECTURE

1992 CAF moves to Railway Exchange Building (called the Santa Fe Building at the time). Great Chicago Flood. Restoration of the Rookery. 1993 CAF partners with Chicago's First Lady Cruises. 1994 The "Loop Tour Train / Round about the Loop" begins. Historic Chicago Stadium is demolished. 1995 CAF and Glessner House each become independent organizations. Navy Pier is redeveloped. CAF's website is launched: architecture.org 1996 CAF opens the John Hancock Center Shop & Tour Center. Philip Johnson lectures at CAF. Unmalling of State Street. Chicago hosts the Democratic National Convention. 1998 City of Chicago launches Great Chicago Spaces and Places Weekend (CAF is the headquarters partner). 2000 Chicago's First Lady Cruises adds a second boat to the river cruise schedule. 2001 CAF mounts the *Chicago Bungalow* exhibition and companion book. CitySpace Gallery opens. City Hall green roof installed.

Even Chicagoans not intimately aware of architecture had reason to be impressed when the Chicago Architecture Foundation had a ribbon-cutting ceremony on May 21, 1992. At the time, board of trustees member Bob Wislow was working at US Equities, which had just received the contract to manage the Railway Exchange Building (named Santa Fe Building for many years). Wislow suggested that his company might bring CAF into the space and reorient the 1904 Daniel Burnham-designed building to attract architecture firms. The idea was inspired and today the Railway Exchange Building is the home of CAF as well as three major firms: Skidmore, Owings & Merrill, VOA and Goettsch Partners. In the Railway Exchange Building CAF enjoyed a larger bookstore, a gallery-lecture hall and offices organized around the building's grand light-filled atrium.

The optimism in moving to Michigan Avenue meant more than a new home filled with history and glazed terra cotta. It was also a sign that the organization had achieved financial stability after a period of much uncertainty. Several executive directors had come and gone since the Glessner House acquisition. A low point came in 1984 when the endowment—never lavish—was drained to almost nothing, largely because $110,000 was consumed to clean and retuckpoint the exterior walls of the historic house. Several board of trustee members even personally guaranteed the bank loan.

CAF had lacked consistent full-time leadership in the 1980s. This caused members of the board of trustees to effectively assume day-to-day management for several years. In addition to Wislow, these trustees included real estate real estate entrepreneur John Buck, attorney Jeffrey Jahns and docent Henry Kuehn. They brought indispensable business skills to the still-growing organization. It took time, but a new executive director was found in 1990. John Engman, who had been a planning officer at the Field Museum, came on board and promised to get his arms around the budget. The ribbon-cutting at the Railway Exchange Building demonstrated that he had done so.

CAF staff and volunteers move from the Monadnock Building into the organization's larger new headquarters in the Railway Exchange Building. March 1992.

(Photos: courtesy Henry Kuehn)

1992-2001

top row, left to right:
Docent Joe Cain leads a neighborhood tour in the Gold Coast. Circa 1983. (Photo: CAF Archives)

Docent Harry Hirsch stops at the Marquette Building on the "Historic Skyscrapers" tour. Circa 1999. (Photo: CAF Archives)

Docent Sylvia Dunbeck on a "Frank Lloyd Wright by Bus" tour which includes stops at Wright's Home and Studio in Oak Park. Circa 1999. (Photo: CAF Archives)

bottom row, left to right:
A docent leads a 2006 tour on the L train around the Loop. This was first introduced as a new tour in 1994. (Photo: CAF Archives)

Docents and husband and wife duo, Don and Joyce Wiberg lead a bike tour along the Chicago River. Circa 1999. (Photo: CAF Archives)

"Grand Illusions by Bus" was introduced as a new tour in 1993 to celebrate the centennial of the World's Columbian Exposition held in Jackson Park. Circa 1999. (Photo: CAF Archives)

EXPANDING TOURS IN THE CITY AND BEYOND

Aside from the budget, Engman and the board quickly took stock of the things that CAF did well, and they set out to capitalize on them. First and foremost, there were tours which were growing every year among Chicago residents and visitors. Tours were a great experience because docents were passionate about architecture and exploring new corners of the city. In 1992, the original Loop tour was divided into two—"Early Skyscrapers" and "Modern and Beyond"— as audience numbers grew along with the list of interesting tall buildings to interpret. Other tours, developed by docents, reached into fascinating neighborhoods in the city and suburbs.

"I always felt that the Bronzeville area had been neglected and its history should be brought to light," said docent Joe LaRue (class of 1980), a South-Sider who wrote and led a tour of this community that was closely tied to the Great Migration of the 1920s. What he showed was a richly layered history with large homes on splendid boulevards, numerous churches and traces of jazz history.

Other new tours went on foot, by bus, by L and even by bicycle, often to well-known landmarks but not always. Wicker Park, Hutchinson Street, Pullman and the Sheffield historic district were among tours conceived and written by docents during this time, most of whom lived in these neighborhoods. The Fine Arts Building, Navy Pier, Grant Park and classic movie palaces were among dozens of other destinations. Some tours were given weekly, others just once or twice a year. In peak periods, reported the 1994 Annual Report, there might be as many as eleven different tours going in a single day.

"Our focus has changed from preservation to architecture education," John Engman told the *Chicago Tribune*. "We're focused on educating people about architecture and urban design as opposed to saving houses." CAF could interpret the city as a museum because the docents made the education real.

Docents had become a force unto themselves. They organized with new self-governing committees and developed the fast-growing tour catalogue.

"You could make a Harvard case study of the way the docent corps developed," said docent Ellen Shubart (class of 2006) who would go on to become docent council president in 2014. New tours were proposed by docents and then approved by the docent tour committee.

A docent's personal interest would often inspire a new tour. In the early 1990s, "New Projects Chicago" toured recently completed buildings such as the R.R. Donnelley Building and the International Terminal at O'Hare. "Grand Illusions by Bus" visited the site of the World's Columbian Exposition during the fair's centennial in 1993. The expansion of neighborhood tours helped create a robust base for CAF membership growth, as local residents wanted to join the organization for its tour benefits. Tour directors—the docents who led efforts to recruit, train and schedule fellow docents, as well as research and write a new tour manual—played an increasingly important role. Neighborhood tours had a remarkable following among CAF's 5,000 existing members. In 1993, more than 70,000 people took a CAF tour led by the organization's 350 docents.

THE AUXILIARY BOARD

Another sign of CAF's strength was fundraising, which took a particularly positive turn in 1992 when the annual gala was held at the Sheraton Chicago. The Riverfront Ball, as it was billed, was a first chance to get a look at the brand-new hotel perched neatly on the river and designed by Solomon Cordwell Buenz. Attendees paid $200 each for the black-tie event that included music by ballroom master Peter Duchin and a silent auction for framed drawings. The organization netted $100,000 for the evening, which showed that the economy was recovering after a rough downturn. And CAF's Auxiliary Board, which put on the annual gala, had emerged strong as well.

The history of the "Aux Board," as it was called, reached back to 1972 when board of trustee member and docent Marian Premer (class of 1971) created this

above, top to bottom:
CAF's 1975 "Rookery Ball" provided guests with the opportunity to dance and mingle in the historic landmark.

Held at the Palmer House Hilton Hotel, the 2009 gala welcomed 600 guests and raised more than $462,000. (Photo: CAF Archives)

right: The Auxiliary Board, here at the 2009 gala continues to play a vital role in supporting the work of CAF. (Photo: CAF Archives)

indispensable branch of CAF advocates. Premer's objective was to raise the organization's profile, which she did early on by inviting descendants of Prairie Avenue families to Glessner House. Among them were docent Barry Sears (class of 1992), whose family was connected to soap and candle manufacturer Joseph Sears, owner of a house once located across the street from the Glessners. There was also Barbara Coleman Donnelley, descendant of the family that built the nearby Joseph Coleman House.

The Aux Board's first gala was in 1974 and was hosted at Glessner House—a "Prairie Avenue Promenade," as it was called—and moved to different significant sites each year thereafter. In 1975, the "Rookery Ball" gave attendees a chance to dance in the lobby of the LaSalle Street landmark. The "Loft Ball" filled a large River North loft space in 1977, when River North was a pioneering new neighborhood. Real estate developers who attended that one saw the "loft movement" up close, some for the first time, and at least one of them went on to become a major CAF benefactor in years to come.

In 1985, the "Carry Me Back" ball was at the South Shore Country Club, a building that was about to undergo a splendid facelift. The gala was chaired by Carry Buck (thus the play-on-words) and became the most successful yet, netting $250,000. It was an important sum for a small organization, but also significant for an unintended reason: the profit equaled almost exactly what was needed for a new roof on Glessner House. Some, not all, assumed that the money would go there. Others insisted Glessner House upkeep had become a drain on financial resources, and that funds should go to educational programs, exhibits and supporting tours. This discussion revealed the organization's divided mission between preservation and education.

above: (left to right) Docent and Manager of Volunteer Services, Barbara Hrbek Gordon; docent Jack McDonald; and docent Pat Talbot celebrate at the "Imperial Ball" in 1995. (Photo: CAF Archives)

opposite: Four members of the first class in 1971 shared the Outstanding Docent of the Year award, given at Docent Appreciation Night in 1995. (left to right) Dev Bowly, Bunny Selig (always in purple, her signature color), Gloria Wallace and Bob Irving. (Photo: CAF Archives)

SHARPENING THE MISSION

Even as the activities of the Chicago Architecture Foundation grew diffuse, the mission remained clear to most members. Henry Kuehn stated this in a "letter to the editor" of the *Docent News* in 1990: "First and foremost, the mission statement of the Foundation has been simplified considerably in order to emphasize architectural education as the fundamental purpose of the CAF." This aspect was not controversial, but then Kuehn went a step further by stating that responsibility for maintaining Glessner House was "subordinate" to the organization's teaching role. It was one of the first public admissions that a break might someday be in order.

Former board of trustees chair Marian Despres wrote to Kuehn in a letter dated February 25, 1992, suggesting additional changes. "Why not start by changing the name 'Chicago Architecture Foundation,'" she wrote, "which is also inadequate, to 'Chicago Architecture Center?' This can be done by simple action of the Board, as has been done before . . . [e]verything comes to the Center. How could anything be more appropriate?"

A separation became more urgent as time passed. A white paper on the subject prepared for the board in 1993 explained that CAF shared responsibility for the Prairie Avenue Historic District with many "key players"—too many, it said. Among them were the City, the Colonial Dames of America who were dedicated to Clarke House and a CAF-affiliated group called Friends of Glessner House. These players "work in a non-cohesive manner resulting in fragmented programming and limited successes," stated the white paper.

After considerable debate and much soul searching, the board of trustees voted to separate CAF from the Glessner House in 1993. The Glessner House incorporated as its own nonprofit using CAF funds as well as proceeds from the sale of the neighboring Kimball and Coleman houses which had been donated to the organization by R. R. Donnelley. While the final break was carefully executed as gently as possible over two years, it was unhappy for some—especially those involved in the Glessner House's rescue some thirty years before. One longtime docent said that "downtown" board members had forgotten CAF's grassroots origins. A *Chicago Tribune* article headlined "Architecture's Broken Foundation" reported on the split in early 1994.

The Glessner House Museum built its own board and, after some false starts, achieved stability. The docent council developed a transition plan and encouraged volunteers to share their skills with both organizations for a period of time. CAF docents assisted with growing a new corps of docents who would interpret the house. To this day, a handful of docents continue to give their time and enthusiasm to both organizations.

As a Victorian era museum, Glessner House found a following among enthusiasts not just of architecture, but of decorative arts and Chicago's Gilded Age. And it found dedicated leadership. "It needed someone who could raise funds and who really loved the house," John Vinci remembered. That person was Bill Tyre, who became the Glessner House executive director in 2007. Tyre had been comptroller of the Society of Architectural Historians and program manager of SAH's historic headquarters, Charnley-Persky House.

NEW LIFE IN THE RAILWAY EXCHANGE BUILDING

Another activity that increased CAF's financial stability was the bookstore. This was not always the case, partially because it had not been well managed, and because its revenues were often consumed by other needs. Henry Kuehn had taken this situation in hand in 1985 after learning that book vendors had cut off shipments because of outstanding bills. Kuehn made a donation to the bookstore with the provision that it be treated as a profit center and that he interview candidates to manage it. Bonita Mall, whose experience was in nonprofit fundraising, got the job and incorporated a wider range of merchandise that went beyond books. Under Mall, retail profits improved, though this was to the dismay of some CAF purists for whom plaster gargoyles and t-shirts diluted what they felt was the bookstore's serious mission.

By the time the ArchiCenter relocated to the Railway Exchange Building, the renamed "Chicago Architecture Foundation Shop" featured colorful merchandise ranging from Frank Lloyd Wright-inspired stained glass to reproductions of Alfonso Ianelli sculpture. Its presence on Michigan Avenue—near the Art Institute and the Chicago Symphony Orchestra—raised visibility immensely. The store had an appealing, contemporary design which was a partial in-kind contribution by board member Vic Vickery and his firm VOA. Results had revenues up to $30,000 a month and sometimes more.

In nearly 30 years, the Chicago Architecture Foundation had acquired a unique body of knowledge about architecture and how to share it with the public. Now it

1992-2001

was eager to show it off, which it did through a series of lectures by significant architects and polished exhibitions. In the late 1990s and early 2000s, CAF hosted architects Phillip Johnson, Daniel Libeskind, Robert Venturi, Cesar Pelli, Ricardo Legorreta and author Witold Rybczynski. The 1993 exhibition, *Put the City Up: Chicago Commercial Architecture, 1892–1992* examined Chicago's Loop and the influence of significant architects on the design of tall buildings. Developed by curator Michael McDonough and docent Pat Talbot (class of 1987) it was geared for a national audience. It opened not in Chicago but at the Smithsonian's National Museum of American History. After hundreds of thousands of people saw it in Washington, it returned to Chicago for a run at the Harold Washington Library. The ArchiCenter was not yet equipped for elaborate exhibits.

The staff grew in this period, and there was never a shortage of topics for exhibits and public programs. *Under Construction* went up in 1994 in the lecture hall gallery which would later be named for the John Buck Company and host weekly lunch-time lectures. This exhibit had 100 construction photos of 13 prominent buildings including the Monadnock Building, the Merchandise Mart and the Sears Tower (now Willis Tower). During the run, Ray Worley, vice president of Morse Diesel, lectured about his experience as general contractor for construction of Sears Tower.

In 1996, the CAF exhibit *Sheltered By Design* was highly anticipated, not only because it explored low-income housing—a timely topic in the city—but because it would be the first show in the atrium gallery of the Railway Exchange Building. Based on a series of *Chicago Tribune* articles by Blair Kamin the year before, the exhibit's narrative began with the promise, and ultimate failure, of post-war high-rise projects in many cities. The story featured smaller scale and more successful approaches in Boston and Cleveland, and the beginnings of scattered-site housing being developed by the Chicago Housing Authority. "The exhibit was an opportunity to have an influence on something that was going to matter to a lot of people," said Bonita Mall, vice president of tours, exhibits and education. Daniel Maguire, board of trustees chair from 1999 to 2001, also highlighted a shift at CAF during these years. In the 1999 annual report, Maguire noted the growing importance of creating new partnerships with individuals and cultural exhibitions in developing exhibitions.

As the organization continued to mount exhibits much as a museum would, it became clear that the most effective programs were those that used Chicago as a backdrop or lens. An excellent (and fondly remembered) major exhibition in 2000 highlighted the city's most widespread type of single-family housing. *The Chicago Bungalow* exhibition was conceived by Charles Shanabruch, a St. Xavier University professor, who wondered what could be done to raise the profile of bungalows. Chicagoans built 80,000 brick bungalows during the 1920s, and yet they were undervalued in terms of both real estate and architecture. Shanabruch first approached Alderman Ginger Rugai to join the effort, and together they imagined the Chicago Bungalow Initiative. Rugai thought the city might get involved, but it required buy-in elsewhere to make it successful. CAF was there almost immediately.

The Chicago Bungalow was curated by Columbia College professor and local historian Dominic Pacyga. He also co-edited, along with Shanaburch, the CAF-commissioned book of the same name. The design made creative use of an

opposite, top to bottom:
The exhibition in the atrium of the Railway Exchange Building, was laid out to resemble the floor plan of a typical Chicago bungalow. Circa 2000. (Photo: CAF Archives)

CAF's 2000 exhibition on the *Chicago Bungalow* highlighted the 80,000 brick bungalows, which make up one-third of the city's single family housing stock. (Photo: courtesy Mati Maldre)

"The Chicago Bungalow exhibit was really seminal. It made people take a new look an architectural resource that was in front of us all the time."

ZURICH ESPOSITO, CAF DIRECTOR
OF EXHIBITS AND PUBLIC PROGRAMS
2001

aluminum modular system in the atrium gallery, arranged to resemble the floor plan of a typical bungalow. "Having a replica of the layout captured something of the lifestyle," remembered Sam Marts, an architect, CAF education volunteer and longtime member of the exhibits committee. The exhibit then went on the road to other venues in Washington D.C., Pasadena, Seattle and Portland.

"This exhibit was really seminal," said Zurich Esposito, director of exhibits and public programs at the time. "It made people take a new look at an architectural resource that was in front of us all the time." The subject had all the right elements. Chicago's so-called "Bungalow Belt" was deeply historical, having expanded with the growth of the Chicago middle class. CAF docents Tom Drebenstedt (class of 1983), David Cholewiak (class of 1999) and Dick Spurgin (class of 1983) also created bus tours for visits to home interiors in bungalow-heavy neighborhoods, mostly on the Southwest and Northwest Sides. Bungalows had a level of craftsmanship that made the building type fashionable once again.

While CAF was becoming a major cultural institution in many ways, it continued to sharpen its focus, and that involved another deaccessioning. Years before, significant archives and artifacts had come to the organization—almost by default— when architectural history was not well-regarded as a valuable cultural resource. That had changed, due largely to CAF's promotion of buildings as a lens on history. Nevertheless, the "invisible museum" lacked some capabilities of a traditional one, and keeping museum-quality objects was one of them.

Parts of the collection went to several other Chicago museums better-equipped to handle them. Items included drawings from Prairie School architects as well as ornament from Sullivan buildings, including the Stock Exchange—donated by Richard Nickel who had salvaged them from the partially-demolished building that collapsed on him in 1972.

GROWTH ON THE RIVER

Of the 50 or so tours offered by CAF, the River Cruise was among the most popular in the early 1990s. But Sally Hess, director of operations at the time, was convinced the tour that docent Bob Irving (class of 1971) had created in 1983 ought to be the premier tour; not only for CAF but for the entire city, which was increasingly attuned to tourism. So in 1993, Hess contacted Holly and Bob Agra, whose family owned the boat company Chicago's First Lady Cruises, with the idea of increasing the river cruise's profile.

The Agras had a long tradition on the lake and river. Bob Agra's grandfather founded Mercury Skyline Cruises in 1935, catering to Chicagoans who needed to cool off by enjoying a lakefront cruise during hot summers. The Agras continued to expand the sightseeing boat business, mostly on the lake, and in 1991 built a stylish new boat; Chicago's First Lady was modeled after the USS Sequoia, the yacht used by Presidents from Herbert Hoover to Jimmy Carter. Handsomely appointed with mahogany and brass, it also had mooring rights at the Michigan Avenue Bridge. (The previous CAF tour boat operated from North Pier Terminal.) It seemed like a very good match for both sides.

Many aspects of the Chicago Architecture Foundation River Cruise aboard Chicago's First Lady Cruises would make it one of the leading tour attractions not

above: Visitors to the exhibition shared memories and photos of life in a Chicago bungalow. Circa 2000. (Photo: CAF Archives)

left to right:

The Chicago Architecture Foundation's partnership with Chicago's First Lady Cruises began in 1993. (Photo: CAF Archives)

By 1997, the Chicago Architecture Foundation River Cruise aboard Chicago's First Lady Cruises was ranked the number-one request fielded by the city's concierge community. Circa 1993. (Photo: Courtesy Chicago's First Lady Cruises)

just in Chicago, but across the country. One advantage was the river's breadth, which provided a full view of the growing list of skyscrapers. And even for dyed-in-the-wool Chicagoans, it was an uncommon view of familiar sights. With Chicago's First Lady, it was not long before the cruise was filled to capacity several times a day. Tourists often said it was first on their lists in Chicago, like Grauman's Chinese Theater in Los Angeles or the Empire State Building in New York. By 1997, it was ranked the number-one request fielded by the city's concierge community.

Few were disappointed. "What was once a shallow stream through a great swamp is now a visitor's gateways for viewing Chicago's internationally acclaimed architecture," wrote a reporter for the *Toronto Globe and Mail.* A *Los Angeles Times* writer was more rhapsodic, "From the boat's top deck, the panorama of the City of the Big Shoulders is unimpeded and . . . inspire[s] awe." An amazing 70,000 people took the river cruise in 1998.

Growth of this sort usually happens by accretion, but a leap forward for this tour happened serendipitously when docent Geoffrey Baer (class of 1987), a behind-the-scenes producer at WTTW Channel 11, began giving tours on the river. Baer had finished a beautiful summer day's tour on the river and stepped ashore where a man and his wife started peppering him with questions. Baer answered each one patiently. They asked him what he did for a living, and when he said he was a producer at Channel 11, the wife poked her husband. The man smiled and admitted he was John McCarter, the new chairman of the board at WTTW.

The next Monday morning, Baer received a memo that he should start work on a documentary that would become *Chicago By Boat,* which aired in 1995. It was the first of a remarkable series of architectural and historical documentaries Baer hosted about countless Chicago neighborhoods and suburbs. These programs have made Baer Chicago's number-one public television celebrity, but to many people, his most important role is still as an active docent at the Chicago Architecture Foundation.

MAKING A MARK IN THE CITY

Broadening the message of architecture had always been an objective of CAF, and it had become increasingly successful both in terms of content and audience. That mission remained prominent when, in 1996, the board of trustees began interviewing for their next executive director. John Engman had accomplished what he was hired to do, which was to stabilize the budget and strengthen programs. Now as trustees David Hart, Jeffrey Jahns, Dan Maguire, Alice Sabl, Lloyd Morgan and Henry Kuehn led the effort to identify candidates, they discussed what the organization needed. It required someone who could expand and reach new audiences, make CAF influential among leaders of Chicago and lead the organization to become a "premier Chicago cultural institution."

An executive recruiter was hired for the assignment and the search began. But as candidates were presented, none seemed just right for the unique CAF position. That was until Lynn Osmond, then living in California, became a candidate. The board of trustees noted Osmond's outgoing and can-do personality and her significant past success in the symphony world. In her previous position she captured new audiences by re-thinking the orchestra's role in the city, and she saw the CAF challenge as analogous. "Much like symphonies, we have a strong traditional audience," she said soon after arriving in Chicago. "But to grow we need to broaden the base among groups whose lives could be enriched by understanding architecture too."

Osmond sensed that architecture could attract many constituencies—young and old, professional and community-based. She came with immense capacity for new ideas, but as a non-architect, she believed she needed to know the subject matter better. For that reason, one of the first things she did after arriving in Chicago was to enter the 1997 docent class. She said that it definitely helped her to imagine CAF's potential impact on the community. And as the first executive director to become a docent, it made her popular in the volunteer corps, still the most important asset of the organization.

BRINGING ARCHITECTURE TO STUDENTS

As cultural offerings grew in the 1990s, so did another element of the organization's mission: education. This role, educating students about the built environment, reached well back in CAF's history, though it was not always prominent. Among the earliest tours, even in the pre-ArchiCenter years, was "Put Your Arms Around a Building," a field trip developed by docent and staff member Jane Lucas (class of 1975). It was in 1992, during Jeffrey Jahns's board of trustees presidency, that CAF first introduced architecture into the lesson plans at four elementary schools in Chicago.

Most transformative in CAF's role as educator was its stewardship of the Newhouse Competition, a once independent project and separate organization which became a part of CAF in 1994. The Newhouse Program and Architecture Competition was the brainchild of Illinois State Senator Richard Newhouse, who was dedicated to opening doors for young people of color. Newhouse worked to correct racial barriers in all areas of society, including architecture. By 1982, the senator was discussing the problems in the profession with friends he knew at Skidmore, Owings & Merrill (SOM). Two SOM partners, Diane Legge Kemp and Robert Wesley, volunteered to help. They began by bringing practicing architects into contact with high school teachers who learned about the skills needed in today's design and construction industries. As the Newhouse Competition took form, Kemp and Wesley oversaw student work and as an end-of-year project, conducted a juried exhibition for hand drawings, models and early Computer Aided Design (CAD) drawings. Even in 1983, its first year, many categories attracted scores of entries. By 1997, the Newhouse Competition drew entries from more than 600 Chicago Public Schools students.

When the Newhouse program was folded into CAF, it brought a new level of volunteerism and donors to the organization. These included John Viera, a Commonwealth Edison executive who brought that company's support to the competition. Viera also became a member of the CAF board of trustees and chair of its education committee for several years. He relished his role in awarding trophies each year to young honorees and seeing many of them on the path to careers. He was also a leader in making corporate financial donations an important source of support for CAF.

Interaction with practicing architects was a critical component and led to stronger architecture programs at many CPS high schools. The effectiveness of these

opposite top and far right: Docent Mary Anne Wencel leads children on an early "Put Your Arms Around a Building" tour, CAF's first field trip for students in the Loop. Circa 1980. (Photo: CAF Archives)

opposite bottom: Students on the "Put Your Arms Around a Building" tour make crayon rubbings to capture the terra cotta pattern on Holabird & Roche's 1895 Marquette Building. Circa 1980. (Photo: CAF Archives)

top: (left) Senator Richard Newhouse stands with Chicago Public Schools students at the awards ceremony after one of the first Newhouse Competitions. Circa 1983. (Photo: CAF Archives)

middle: Newhouse Competition projects— drawings, physical models, digital models and renderings—continue to be juried by teams of local architects who determine the winners in various divisions. Circa 2002. (Photo: CAF Archives)

bottom, left to right:
Lee Weintraub, architect and CAF volunteer, served as the chairman of the Newhouse Competition for ten years. Circa 1998. (Photo: CAF Archives)

Trustee John Viera (left) relished the opportunity to present trophies to the Newhouse Competition award winners for many years. In 2010, Lane Technical High School student Fariha Wajid (right) received an internship at Studio Gang Architects. (Photo: CAF Archives)

above, top to bottom:
Architect Sam Marts taught color theory and rendering at Saturday Studios for many years, as Chicago Public High School students prepared for the Newhouse Competition. Circa 2000. (Photo: CAF Archives)

Newhouse Competition alumn Darryl Crosby spoke to high school students at the 1991 awards ceremony, as architect Stanley Tigerman looked on. During his college years at UIC, Crosby worked for Tigerman. (Photo: CAF Archives)

above right: As a winner in the Newhouse Competition, student Mario Romero of Lane Technical High School was awarded a summer internship at Smith + Gill Architects. Circa 2009. (Photo: CAF Archives)

relationships was illustrated by architect Lee Weintraub, who began volunteering in the early 1990s and was chair of the Newhouse Competition for ten years. Involvement also meant working with high school teachers, Weintraub said, who were not typically connected to the profession in tangible ways to teach up-to-date techniques. He, and other architects volunteering with the program, gave weekend workshops for teachers and students to help them learn the profession's current practices.

Weintraub was personally enriched by this work and extremely gratified that a series of his employers supported it. "Jack Train was the first one who taught me the value of mentoring," he said. "It was important interacting with real people, not just other architects." Weintraub followed in kind and recruited younger colleagues to get involved in Newhouse, and that included Joel Berman, whom he supervised when both worked at Lester B. Knight and Associates. So began Berman's long relationship with the organization and also his mentoring of student interns at Knight and later at VOA. "I came to meet some really driven young people," Berman said.

The tenacity that Berman witnessed was hardly isolated. Many students went on to obtain architecture and engineering degrees and to have sterling careers in design. Darryl Crosby was a Newhouse Competition winner in 1986, the year he graduated from Robeson High School. He went on to earn an architecture degree at the University of Illinois at Chicago (UIC) and later worked for architect Stanley Tigerman before opening his own practice. Fernando Espinosa also earned an architecture degree at UIC and eventually an MBA. He worked at Perkins + Will and later became a project manager with the City of Chicago. Another example was Mario Romero who entered the Newhouse Competition as a sophomore at Lane Technical High School. He won with a project for a CAD-designed residence for people with disabilities. The award earned Romero an internship at Adrian Smith + Gordon Gill Architects. He later went off to architecture school. Throughout his school years he said, "every time I had a break I asked to come back." Eight years later, Romero got a full-time position at Smith + Gill where today he mentors Newhouse honorees who come in as interns—as young and eager as he once was.

Recent public program themes at the Chicago Architecture Foundation

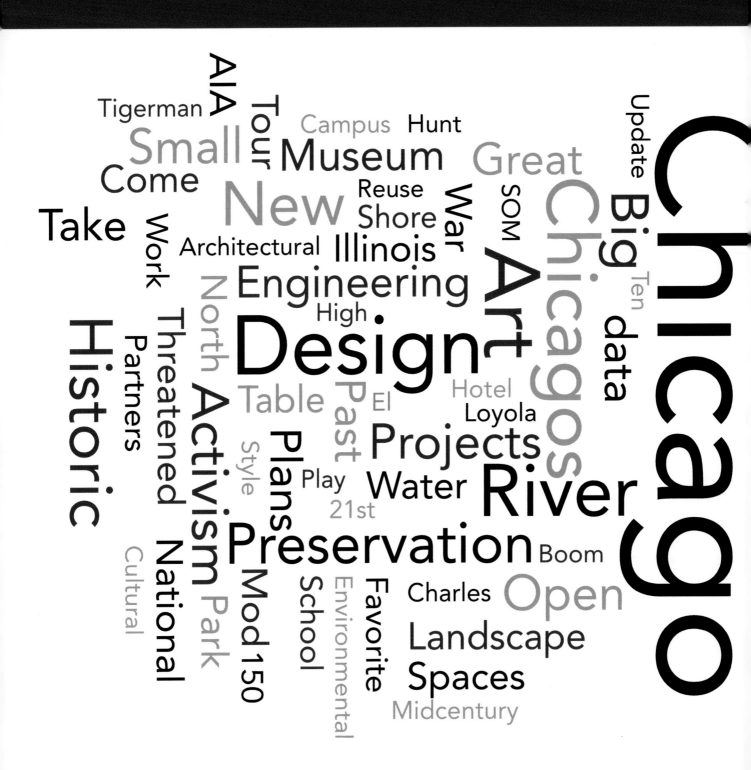

Tigerman AIA Campus Hunt Update Chicago
Small Tour Museum Great Big
Come New Reuse Shore War SOM Chicagos Ten data
Take Work Architectural Illinois Art
Engineering High
North Design Hotel
Historic Partners Threatened Table Past El Loyola Projects
Style Plans Play Water River
21st Boom
Activism Park Preservation
Cultural National Mod 150 School Environmental Favorite Charles Open
Landscape
Spaces
Midcentury

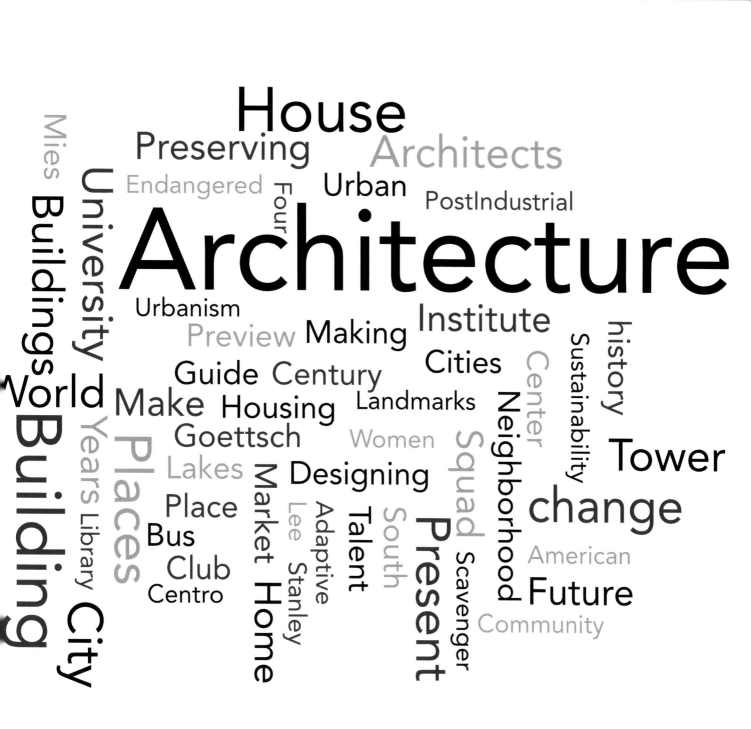

CHAPTER FOUR

SEEING THE WORLD THROUGH ARCHITECTURE

2002 Graphic designers from Thirst redesign CAF's logo and branding. CAF first publishes the award-winning K-8 curriculum, *Schoolyards to Skylines: Teaching with Chicago's Amazing Architecture.* 2003 *Invisible Cities: Planning for Chicago's Future* exhibition. 2004 *Big & Green* exhibition. The Stein Ray Harris Patron of the Year Award is established. CAF initiates a high school curriculum for CPS. 2005 CAF partners with the American Architectural Foundation to launch the Architecture and Design Education Network (A+DEN). *Schoolyards to Skylines* awarded National AIA Honor Award for Collaborative Achievement. Crown Hall exterior is restored. 2006 CAF celebrates its 40th anniversary. Mission statement: "The Chicago Architecture Foundation is dedicated to advancing public interest and education in architecture and related design." 78 different tours are offered. *Schoolyards to Skylines* sales reach over 1,200 books around the world. Listening devices are introduced on downtown walking tours with capacity for foreign language tours in French, Spanish, German and Japanese. Chicago's First Lady Cruises adds a third boat. CAF celebrates in the city-wide 150th anniversary of Louis Sullivan's birth. 2007 CAF publishes the first high school architecture textbook in the nation, *The Architecture Handbook: A Student Guide to Understanding Buildings.* The Newhouse Program and Architecture Competition celebrates its 25th year and attracts over 1,500 high school students annually. 2008 CAF launches *Family Studio Sundays.* The Hem C. Gupta lecture with London-based architect David Adjaye brings in an audience of 412 people. CAF reaches an audience of over 476,000 for various programming, including lectures, exhibitions, youth education, retail, and most importantly, tours. 240,000 go on a CAF tour. CAF reaches a membership of 6,500. Operating budget is $10.8M.

2009 CAF celebrates the city-wide centennial of Burnham and Bennett's 1909 Plan of Chicago. *Chicago Model* exhibition opens. Association of Architecture Organizations hosts inaugural conference in Chicago. Launch of CAF's social media presence on Twitter and Facebook. *The Architecture Handbook* awarded National AIA Honor Award for Collaborative Achievement. 2010 "Elevated Architecture" tour is launched in partnership with the CTA. "85 Tours Challenge" social media campaign is completed on December 16th. 2011 First annual Open House Chicago welcomes more than 23,000 visitors. Stanley Tigerman assembled *Design on the Edge: Visionary Architects Reimagine Neighborhoods* exhibition with five renowned architects.

Architecture touched everyone in 2001 the day the World Trade Center towers were destroyed in New York. Beyond the unspeakable catastrophe of the attack, many Americans had relentless questions about what happened and what that meant for the future of skyscrapers and cities.

By the following spring, an exhibit of photographs of the World Trade Center by Camilo Jose Vergara—scenes from construction to destruction—went on display highlighting architecture as the centerpiece of a moving tribute. Among lectures on the buildings, Skidmore, Owings & Merrill partner John Zils lectured at CAF about his experience at ground zero where he joined scores of fellow structural engineers in the rescue and recovery. Zils discussed the careful untangling of debris and also answered questions about the collapse of the towers, which was caused by heat and weakened columns in the area of impact.

CAF kept a full calendar of events in this period, and many exhibits seemed more attuned than ever to the concerns of the times. In 2003, *Invisible Cities: Planning for Chicago's Future* challenged leading architecture firms to gaze into the future, much as Daniel Burnham had a century before. Perkins + Will imagined a green belt through the middle of the city by building a roof over the Kennedy Expressway. Joe Valerio and Linda Searle proposed a technology park and inter-modal transportation hub in suburban Berkeley. The ideas were visionary, thus impractical at the time, but they addressed problems of air quality and infrastructure that seemed only more urgent 10 years later.

None of the ideas in *Invisible Cities* entered the political realm, but there remained a desire at CAF to generate interest in social questions where the built environment was at stake. In 2006, CAF partnered with Architecture For Humanity in a three-part lecture series entitled "Rebuilding and Re-envisioning the Gulf Coast" which debated varied approaches to the Hurricane Katrina response. On one memorable panel, John Norquist, New Urbanism proponent of large-scale traditional planning, debated Reed Kroloff, who was dean of architecture at Tulane University and a modernist who argued for an organic approach.

Kroloff, former editor of *Architecture* magazine, was something of a regular at CAF and later moderated a highly successful symposium, "Spotlight on Shrinking Cities." Co-sponsored with the American Architecture Foundation (AAF) and the Chicago Chapter of the American Institute of Architects (AIA), it addressed the decline of major cities. As for causes, participants blamed a variety of demons, and Kroloff, by then director of Cranbrook Academy outside Detroit, noted that trouble in many cities was due to one-note economies. "But shrinking is not dying," he said, citing modern Pittsburgh, Pennsylvania and Chattanooga, Tennessee.

One sign of CAF's maturity as an institution was audience research conducted in this period, primarily through surveys of tours and programs. Sustainability and residential architecture were themes that came up consistently, and speakers were signed up to meet the need. The staff ideas were topical and up-to-date. "We had the freedom to try everything," said Barbara Gordon who interacted closely with visitors and volunteers during her 20 years at CAF. Gordon's understanding of the public's interests, plus her deep roster of available public-program participants, became invaluable assets of the organization. She began in 1995 shortly after earning an education degree, became a docent, and ran the docent program as

manager of public programs and volunteers until becoming vice president of program operations.

"We found speakers who could show how architecture mattered," Gordon said. Around 2008, for example, CAF hosted presentations of the Chicago 2016 Olympic bid, a controversial issue with the public. CAF also offered a bus tour of potential sites to inform architects eager to get in on the massive projects that would have happened. By 2010, CAF's role as moderator inspired the "Chicago Debates" series. Topics included "The Malling of Chicago," and "Designing a Casino for Chicago." In 2011, the series tackled the battle over preserving Bertrand Goldberg's Prentice Hospital. These debates were held in surprisingly apt venues—the one on Prentice was held at Dick's Last Resort, a restaurant in Goldberg's most famous masterpiece, Marina City.

TEACHING THE LANGUAGE OF BUILDINGS

A different aspect of architectural thinking was reflected in another important activity of the organization: how architecture could be used in the classrooms of elementary and high schools. For years, CAF staff had witnessed the power of architecture in the classroom but also its limitations. It made perfect sense that it could be used as a teaching tool for many subjects, but transmitting this message to thousands of students, with a small CAF education staff, was a long-term

above: Edward Lifson (center right) of WBEZ moderated the "Chicago Debates" series, including this one on "The Malling of Chicago" which centered around proposed changes near Wrigley Field.

challenge. The organization refocused its efforts on field trips, which brought students downtown, and in curricular development to assist teachers in using architecture in their own classrooms.

As early as the 1970s, Loop tours for school groups showed that even the youngest students could be excited by buildings. In the mid-1990s, docents and education staff worked with teachers to develop "Structures: The Secrets of Skyscrapers," a field trip that introduced structural elements (column, beam, cantilever, etc.) to third and fourth graders through hands-on informal learning and Loop explorations. Docent Evelyn Goltz (class of 1997) worked with education staff to develop "Structures" and she served as the tour director for many years. In 1999 a redesigned "Student Loop Tour" introduced 10 Loop buildings and 10 key architectural themes (design, technology, materials, ornamentation, etc.) to fifth through eighth grade students.

In 1996, CAF published *Building Your Future* to introduce elementary school students to architecture with lessons for teachers. The organization found that distributing the book widely in schools represented a difficult hurdle. Especially in public schools, state and district-wide benchmarks in reading and math were strict. But educators needed more specifics about *how* architecture could be applied to their required lessons or grade levels.

In 1999, the organization began forging lasting relationships with many educators in Chicago and the suburbs when Jean Linsner began as director of youth education. Linsner developed a series of popular year-round professional development workshops for teachers. These classes demonstrated that many educators were intensely interested in architecture, but they needed specific how-to steps and connections to their required curricula.

With good experience behind it, CAF undertook the challenge of writing a new teacher-tested resource. In 2000, education specialist Jen Masengarb came to CAF with training as an architect and architectural historian, as well as classroom teaching experience. By 2002, she authored *Schoolyards to Skylines: Teaching With Chicago's Amazing Architecture* with help from Linsner. Designed for teachers of kindergarten through eighth grade, it was a step-by-step guide of how to use Chicago's well-known and vernacular buildings, places and events as tools for teaching the core subjects. Lessons grew out of the state and local academic standards and explored topics such as the Great Chicago Fire, immigrant architecture, movable bridges, skyscrapers, sustainability, Frank Lloyd Wright's windows, Chicago bungalows, terra cotta and the 1924 Tribune Tower design competition.

Supported by CAF's intensive teacher training and workshops, public and private schools began to use *Schoolyards to Skylines* in their lessons. Therese Laslo, a teacher at De Diego Community Academy in Humboldt Park, was one of a dozen teachers who served on the educator advisory team for *Schoolyards to Skylines*. She found that architecture gave children "a way of seeing the world through the many cultures that the kids confront every day." Laslo had long found buildings a useful tool. Now she had a vocabulary and classroom strategies for describing churches, skyscrapers and three-flats.

The success of *Schoolyards to Skylines* could be measured in sales. By 2013, the 500-page book was on its fourth printing and used by educators, architects

right: Docents and staff created new field trips specifically aimed at younger audiences. Tour director and docent Evelyn Goltz leads third and fourth graders in a "Structure: The Secret of Skyscrapers" field trip. Students learn first about the forces and structures that hold up buildings and then explore the Loop. Circa 2006. (Photo: Anne Evans, CAF Archives)

above left: Chicago teachers Fonda Baldwin (left) and Cary Williams (right) celebrate at the book launch party for *Schoolyards to Skylines: Teaching with Chicago's Amazing Architecture* in 2002. They served on the 20-member educator advisory board which field-tested all 47 lessons in CAF's K-8th grade teacher resource book. (Photo: Anne Evans, CAF Archives)

above right: Schoolyards to Skylines lessons used the local built environment as a tool for teaching the core subjects in social science, science, mathematics, language arts and fine arts. Students in this fifth grade science class used CAF's lesson on the physics of Chicago's movable bridges. Circa 2004. (Photo: Jen Masengarb, CAF Archives)

and after-school architecture programs in all 50 states and 16 countries. While the book was intended for Chicago, its pedagogy and strategies of teaching with the built environment were soon adopted around the world.

In 2007, CAF increased its partnership with CPS by publishing a textbook for high school students and teachers. *The Architecture Handbook: A Student Guide to Understanding Buildings* was the first architecture text for high school students in the nation. With Rehbein serving as project coordinator and Masengarb as author, the pair embarked on a three-year project with more than 100 volunteer advisors comprised of Chicago's design community, CPS educators and teen advisory teams. The goal was to shift CPS's drafting curriculum from an emphasis on replication and repetition (and replace the 1951 booklet still used in CPS classrooms) to one of architectural literacy that focused on innovation and creativity.

The 300-page student edition and accompanying teacher edition met the needs of teens and educators—and the goals of the architectural profession—by teaching design concepts and technical drawing through lessons about the home, a familiar building type to all students. Chapters on topics such as the block plan, site plan, floor plan, elevation and section used a local sustainable home as a case study and compared 10 well-known residential buildings around the world—including Glessner House.

The success of *The Architecture Handbook* came about not just because of CAF's ambition to educate more students, but also through a shift in CPS. The Education to Careers initiative was being pushed by Arne Duncan, CEO of CPS who would later become Secretary of Education under President Barack Obama. Duncan brought in lawyer Jill Wine-Banks to run Education to Careers with the goal of making high schools more responsive to employers' needs. Wine-Banks enthusiastically endorsed *The Architecture Handbook*. Chicago high school architecture programs were placed under a trained architect, Melissa Barbier, who was involved in the book's content and was instrumental in helping it become the official text in CPS. "For the first time, we were introducing design thinking skills," Barbier said.

High school educators across the country quickly found the lessons and hands-on activities in *The Architecture Handbook* helpful in shifting in their own curriculum away from a drafting focus to one that instead introduced students to architectural design. Within eight years, the text was in use in 350 high schools across the U.S. and 18 other countries. And following on the heels of a 2005 win for *Schoolyards to Skylines*, *The Architecture Handbook* was also awarded a National Honor Award for Collaborative Achievement from the American Institute of Architects in 2009.

Also connected to the CAF-CPS relationship was the Taliesin Fellowship, where top students visited the architecture school that Frank Lloyd Wright established in Wisconsin and later in Arizona. Chicago teens were among the first high school students invited to Taliesin, for a week at a time, to work on projects in a true design studio setting with fellows. The program was a credit to CAF's power to collaborate with important architectural partners. In this case, it came about through the contacts of Auxiliary Board member Sandra Dubos who was also a member of the Taliesin board. "CAF has such a wide range of audiences," Rehbein said in explaining this success. "It was exciting to make connections that could create an innovative program like this."

opposite left, top to bottom:
Until 2007, when CAF's *The Architecture Handbook: A Student Guide to Understanding Buildings* was published, architecture classes in Chicago Public Schools used this 1951 booklet. (CAF Archives)

Lane Tech College Prep high school student Ricardo Escutia was one of 7 teens who met at CAF each Monday after school for an entire year to test more than 75 activities in CAF's *The Architecture Handbook*. Circa 2007. (Photo: Jen Masengarb, CAF Archives)

opposite right, top to bottom:
CAF published the first high school architecture textbook in the country in 2007. Here, (left to right) Jean Linsner, CAF director of youth education; Jen Masengarb author and CAF education specialist; Jill Wine-Banks, Chief Officer of Career and Technical Education, Chicago Public Schools; and Krisann Rehbein, project coordinator and CAF education specialist celebrate at the book's launch party. (Photo: Anne Evans, CAF Archives)

In developing *The Architecture Handbook*, CAF brought together more than 100 design professionals and high school educators who served as advisors. Here, Joe Cliggott (left) of Goettsch Partners and Ron Miller (right) of Schurz High School discuss the book's lessons following an advisory meeting. Circa 2006. (Photo: Jen Masengarb, CAF Archives)

The growth of the education department had another significant success in 2009 when the National Endowment for the Humanities awarded CAF with a coveted grant from its Landmarks of American History and Culture program. It was for $170,000 and provided stipends for 80 teachers from around the country (from "the Bronx to Baltic, South Dakota" and beyond) to come and discover what CAF had learned about teaching through architecture. The program was repeated over four additional summers, and CAF's two published curricular resources became key workshop tools as teachers received copies to use in their own classrooms. "This was a big milestone that helped move CAF from being solely a local organization for K-12 education to one with national impact," Masengarb said. These workshops inspired many other organization activities.

EXHIBITING THE SOUL OF THE CITY

Traditionally, museums of all kinds make their greatest impact in the area of informal education. This inspired more exhibit space for CAF, and in 2001, the CitySpace gallery was built out in a Jackson Boulevard storefront adjacent to the Railway Exchange Building atrium. CitySpace served other functions beyond exhibits: a small downtown model donated by SOM, a more public window to

above, top to bottom:
CAF's workshops equipped educators with the skills to use their own communities and buildings as a tool for teaching the core subjects. Circa 2013. (Photo: Jen Masengarb, CAF Archives)

CAF's first model of downtown, donated by SOM for the CitySpace Gallery off Jackson Boulevard, provided docents with the opportunity to share a new perspective. Here, docent Janet Forte starts her tour with an orientation at the model. Circa 2004. (Photo: Anne Evans, CAF Archives)

above right: Over five summers, 400 teachers from across the country came to CAF as part of a National Endowment for the Humanities-sponsored week-long workshop on "The American Skyscraper: Transforming Chicago and the Nation." 2013 (Photo: Anne Evans, CAF Archives)

CAF, an orientation center on Chicago history with interactive screens and an information counter. CitySpace was possible in part through a capital campaign that resulted in the first of many naming opportunities for facilities: the John Buck Company Lecture Hall, the Eric Multhauf Lunchtime Lectures and the Elizabeth Morse Learning Studio which expanded more formal education activities.

With added facilities came programs of greater depth, designed largely by chief curator Ned Cramer, formerly an editor at *Architecture* magazine. Cramer came to CAF in 2002 and brought public engagement to new levels. Illustrative if not typical was a competition and exhibit for plans to restore St. Boniface, an abandoned historic church on the near west side. For the "charrette," as it was called, the Archdiocese provided stipends for the competition teams. Designs came from four leading firms—Booth Hansen, Studio Gang, annex/5 (part of Epstein and Sons) and the eventual winner, Brininstool + Lynch. Schemes focused on housing and social service, and many ideas were taken up by proposals from private developers, though the 1902 Romanesque building was still awaiting its fate in 2016.

Other programs and exhibits showed that Cramer and his staff were attuned to new trends and eager to introduce them. In 2005, *New Federal Architecture: The Face of a Nation* featured high-design in government buildings of recent years. All of the buildings in the exhibition were designed and build under the steward-ship of the General Services Administration's chief architect Ed Feiner, who lectured at CAF during the exhibit's run. Also speaking during the show was Thom Mayne of the Los Angeles firm Morphosis, designer of a striking exo-skeleton of a building for the National Oceanic and Atmospheric Administration (NOAA) outside Washington, DC. Mayne's appearance, at that year's Hem C. Gupta lecture, was prescient as the architect was awarded the Pritzker Prize hardly a month after his visit to CAF.

In the months and years that followed, CAF would continue to host influential thinkers, critics and designers who lectured about their recent work. In 2005

London-based architect Will Alsop shared his lively view of contemporary architecture. Urban critic and visionary Charles Landry lectured at CAF in 2006 on what it takes to create world-class city. In 2008, the Gupta lecture series brought British architect David Adjaye, who spoke passionately on "Making Public Buildings." In 2009, CAF hosted a groundbreaking event that brought together four of the nation's most prominent architectural critics to imagine the future of our cities and debate the role of design. Nearly 350 people heard Blair Kamin of the *Chicago Tribune*, Paul Goldberger of *The New Yorker*, Christopher Hawthorne of the *Los Angeles Times* and Sarah Williams of *The New Republic* discuss the changing notions of a model, livable city.

Cramer's four-year tenure at CAF will be remembered for cutting-edge topics and speakers. Another eye-catching exhibit in 2005 was *5 Architects* highlighting five women in, or approaching, the top rank of the profession. Carol Ross Barney and Jeanne Gang, both of Chicago, were featured. Cramer pointed out that the exhibit title played on a 1972 book of the same name that featured five architects— all male—and whose work was defined as a unified approach to architecture. "The present exhibition, by contrast, illustrates the diversity and collaborative spirit of contemporary architecture," Cramer wrote.

Sustainable architecture was also examined through *Big & Green: Toward Sustainable Architecture in the 21st Century,* organized by the National Building Museum and brought to CAF in 2004. The exhibit used the Swiss Re tower in London as a harbinger for its "breathing" glass exterior. A sprawling office park in California illustrated innovative wastewater strategies. *Big and Green* was accompanied by a local exhibit, *Chicago Green,* which included plans for Helmut Jahn's Mercy Lakefront SRO. Both exhibits made clear that a healthy environment depended in part on well-designed architecture. Less obvious was the more recent idea that higher density made many technologies more efficient.

Artist Alexander Calder's model of the *Flamingo* sculpture in Chicago's Federal Plaza served as the centerpiece for *New Federal Architecture,* CAF's exhibition which opened in 2005. (Photo: Anne Evans, CAF Archives)

above, left to right:
In 2008, CAF presented *Do We Dare Squander Chicago's Great Architectural Heritage,* an exhibition which highlighted the successes— such as Glessner House—and struggles of the city's preservation movement. (Photo: Anne Evans, CAF Archives)

Big and Green, a traveling exhibition organized by the National Building Museum came to CAF in 2004 and highlighted new sustainable architecture across Chicago and the country. (Photo: Anne Evans, CAF Archives)

bottom row, left to right:
Renowned British architect David Adjaye (center) spoke to a large audience in 2008 as part of CAF's Hem C. Gupta lecture series. (Left to right) Lynn Osmond, CAF President and CEO; Raj Gupta, Environmental Systems Design, Inc. CEO and CAF board of trustees member; David Adjaye; Hem C. Gupta; John Syvertsen, OWP/P President and past chair CAF board of trustees. (Photo: Anne Evans, CAF Archives)

CAF's 2004 exhibition, popular with Chicagoans who remembered the 1933–1934 World's Fair as children, *A Century of Progress* featured never-before-seen images. The Museum of Science and Industry loaned architects' original color renderings, while the Chicago Park District shared archival photos of the Fair. (Photo: Anne Evans, CAF Archives)

Walt Eckenhoff, CAF board of trustees chair from 2003 to 2005, noted that *Big & Green* was CAF's largest exhibition to date. Producing it with the City of Chicago and the National Building Museum, it highlighted CAF's ability to form effective partnerships. Eckenhoff recalls that it also "helped cast an early public focus on the role of sustainability in Chicago and its influence on design in general."

While contemporary architecture had become prominent at CAF, so was architectural history which was highlighted in a 2005 exhibit, *Learning from North Lawndale.* It looked at the rich history of one of Chicago's most underserved neighborhoods and its rapid change in the 20th century from a predominantly Jewish population to an African-American community. Highlighted was the story of rehabbed historic greystones and their role in neighborhood value and reinvestment.

In 2008, curator Greg Dreicer, who came to CAF from the National Building Museum in Washington, D.C., organized *Do We Dare Squander Chicago's Great Architectural Heritage?,* which recounted the successes and failures of the local preservation movement. The lengthy title of the exhibit came from a picket sign carried by Richard Nickel in 1961 while protesting the imminent demolition of the Garrick Theater. (Nickel is a well-regarded figure in the preservation movement. He died in 1972 while photographing and salvaging ornament from Adler and Sullivan's partially demolished Chicago Stock Exchange Building.) CAF's pivotal role in saving the Glessner House in 1966 was also highlighted.

CHICAGO MODEL

As exhibits reached new levels of quality, President and CEO Lynn Osmond was determined to develop something striking for the centennial celebration of Daniel Burnham and Edward Bennett's iconic 1909 *Plan of Chicago*. Inspired by the success of the smaller-scale city model on display in CitySpace and sprawling models seen in Shanghai and Paris, Osmond imagined a way to illustrate what 100 years had wrought. The result was *Chicago Model City,* which opened in 2009 and filled the entire central section of the atrium gallery. In a period of digital-centric exhibits, a physical model was seen as old-school by some. But like similar projects around the world, the Chicago model became a landmark in itself. Driecer shared an enthusiasm for the value of teaching with physical models and sought creative ways to create CAF's most ambitious atrium exhibition on a modest budget.

The model was a three-dimensional map with more than a thousand buildings in recognizable detail on some forty square blocks, located on a 320-square-foot stage. In broad strokes, it showed the context of central neighborhoods such as the Loop and the river corridors. It revealed the relative density of less-well-known parts to the south, and even suggested the direction of urban growth.

Aside from its urbanistic interest, the model was fascinating for the way it was made, using 3D printing, a relatively new technology at the time, to create detailed hollow resin buildings with digital information collected from countless sources. Digital design files of many buildings were loaned by architects, other scans were taken from airplanes. Data was consolidated by a Chicago-based model maker, Columbia Model and Exhibit Works, and the pieces were fabricated by several donors with state-of-the-art 3D printers, such as Baxter Healthcare, DSM Somos and Molex.

Catherine Tinker, president of Columbia Model, explained that the Chicago model's scale, one inch to fifty feet, was larger than most of those in other cities, the better to draw visitors in. "In this one you can look down the streets and imagine yourself within the model," Tinker said. The effect on visitors to CAF was evident. More than 71,000 people saw it in six months, which was its planned run in the atrium gallery. After that, it was extended permanently. "We could never have predicted what a success it has been," Osmond said.

THE DOCENT CULTURE GROWS

As CAF became identified with exhibits, lectures and school programs, the docent program also grew. Docents remained vigorously independent, but they were also increasingly integrated with staff and wider organizational goals and initiatives. Many new tours were created between 2003 and 2006, largely the result of an extensive survey of the docent corps organized by docent Myra Gary (class of 1999). Docent Robin Simon (class of 1997) wrote and analyzed the survey which asked docents to consider which buildings, eras, styles, themes, people or events in

top to bottom:

Staff from Columbian Model and Exhibit Works installs CAF's 3D-printed Chicago model. Originally conceived in 2009 as a temporary exhibition, the model's popularity with the public led CAF curators to make it a centerpiece for all large exhibitions in the years that followed. (Photo: Anne Evans, CAF Archives)

During a special exhibition opening in 2009, Mayor Richard M. Daley (right) receives a detailed 3D-printed model of City Hall from CAF board of trustees chair John DiCiurcio. (Photo: Anne Evans, CAF Archives)

Chicago's built environment were missing from the existing roster of tours. Over the next several years, new tours such as the "Reliance Building," "Downtown Deco" along LaSalle Street and "Treasures of Culture and Commerce" along State Street and Michigan Avenue grew out of this research.

By the middle of the decade, docents had also developed a tour around the wildly popular book, *Devil in the White City*, which brought the 1893 World's Columbian Exposition and Daniel Burnham's role in the Fair to life. And even before Millennium Park opened in 2004, docents created a tour of the park's sculpture, gardens and pavilions—Chicago's new downtown jewel.

Docents watched market forces, too, and surveys of tour takers led to new lunchtime tours—an hour or so focused on individual landmarks such as the Monadnock Building, the Rookery or the Chicago Board of Trade. "These were great tours because you could get up very close to the buildings," said Jason Neises. Neises began on staff as the tour coordinator, became a docent (class of 2001) and later worked as manager of volunteer services before going on to become vice president of tours and guest relations.

In 2009, the Myra Gary Award for Tour Development was endowed by Jim Gary to honor the life of his late wife. The award recognizes a CAF docent for excellence in the development of a new tour. Docent Mary Jo Hoag (class of 2007) was the first recipient, honoring her creation of the "Graceland Cemetery: Women of Influence" tour which celebrated the lives and work of women in Chicago's early history. It was one of many new tours that would symbolize the reach of CAF docents into untapped histories, places and people.

As the number of tours and tour departures continued to increase to meet public demand, especially on the river, docents rose to the challenge. In these years, tour director Syma Dodson (class of 1992) served as a determined advocate for docents of CAF's River Cruise aboard Chicago's First Lady and substantially grew the numbers of these volunteers. Docents worked with staff to continually refine tours and the catalogue of offerings. They seized every opportunity to create tours

below: Docents eagerly created new tours to share significant, but overlooked Chicago structures not previously in the tour roster. Docent Peggy Dwyer interprets Louis Sullivan's Carson Pirie Scott Building on the "Historic Treasures of Culture and Commerce" tour. Circa 2003. (Photos: Anne Evans, CAF Archives)

opposite top: Even before Millennium Park officially opened in 2004, CAF docents had developed a new tour of the spaces and art in the park. Docent Huette Kaplan highlights the Pritzker Pavilion, designed by Frank O. Gehry and Associates. Circa 2005. (Photo: Anne Evans, CAF Archives)

opposite bottom, left to right:
With the popularity of *The Devil in the White City*, Erik Larson's 2004 book, docent Chris Multhauf and others developed—with permission from Larson—a new bus tour of the same name. It focused on the architectural stories of the 1893 World's Fair. Circa 2007. (Photo: Anne Evans, CAF Archives)

"Downtown Deco" tour focused on the opulent 1920s buildings along LaSalle Street and quickly became a popular addition to CAF's roster of tours. Here, docent Charles McLaughlin highlights an Art Deco interior. Circa 2010. (Photo: Anne Evans, CAF Archives)

that would highlight the latest developments and forgotten stories of Chicago. Strong docent committees continued—for training, developing new tours, enrichment, continuing education, responding to occasional complaints and other aspects of docent self-government.

To assure quality, a peer review process was instituted with a strictness that might have surprised some volunteers if not devised by the docents themselves. The peer-review idea actually reached back to the late 1980s when docent Louise Haack (class of 1988) proposed, as she termed it, a "mutual observation society." New docents had always been certified by veteran docents for each tour they gave, but in the new peer review process launched in 2005, every docent's tour—key talking points, tour logistics and how well they related to their audience—was evaluated every three years. "With few exceptions, docents welcomed the feedback from their peers," said docent Jane Buckwalter (class of 1998 and docent council president from 2001 to 2003) who led these efforts along with Mike Cohen (class of 1998).

Beyond this admittedly complex committee structure, docents were distinguished by the sheer quality of the individuals who made up the corps. Many were retired professionals and educators. One had been a regional planner, another an FBI agent, another a university administrator, yet another was a vice president at a large museum. "Docents tend to be super-achievers, said docent Kathleen Carpenter (class of 2006). They are accustomed to making a difference in anything they do."

Each docent brought the experience of a career and a lifetime in Chicago to the organization. Docent Ron Tevonian (class of 1999) brought digital skills, first creating a website for his 1999 class that soon expanded to all docents. Tevonian's site became the first internal tool for electronic communication and knowledge sharing among the docent corps. This, combined with the advent of a digital scheduling system (rather than a monthly mailed newsletter and paper tour signup sheet), increased the efficiency and nimbleness with which the organization could schedule tours— and enabled docents to schedule themselves.

Docent Mary Jo Hoag created "Graceland Cemetery: Women of Influence" tour which took a new look at familiar place, celebrating the lives and work of women in Chicago's early history. Circa 2010. (Photo: Anne Evans, CAF Archives)

"Seeing hidden places, private spaces, widens the world for us."

The dedication, longevity of service years, tour development skills and commitment of CAF docents has become the gold-standard among volunteer organizations across the country. More than 30 percent of the 450-member docent corps routinely give an additional 20, 40 or even 60 tours—well beyond the required 10 tours per year. And docents treasure the unique experiences they gain while meeting visitors from around the world and sharing the city's architecture. "No two tours are alike," said docent Tom Carmichael (class of 2007), current tour director of the CAF River Cruise aboard Chicago's First Lady Cruises. "And depending upon the group, a tour could be like gathering in your living room with the river all around you."

OUTSIDE CAF'S COMFORT ZONE

The will to reach beyond controlled certainties may be an architect's most valuable trait. That was CAF's driving force as it continued to venture out —both geographically to new parts of the city and suburbs and with new partners, some of which did not previously consider themselves much interested in architecture.

It began years before with neighborhood tours created by docents. "One of the real success stories of CAF in the last twenty years is how it has instilled pride in many neighborhoods," said Walt Eckenhoff, board of trustees chair from 2003 to 2005. In fact, the potential for this success was limitless, and with that in mind CAF inaugurated Neighborhood Voices in 2010, partnering with community organizations in underserved areas across the city. With CAF expertise and training, residents learned how to identify their community's architectural assets, develop their own tours and share the pride they felt for their neighborhood.

Krisann Rehbein, then manager of community partnerships and docent (class of 2004), Hallie Rosen, director of volunteers and docent (class of 2010) and docent Tom Drebenstedt (class of 1986) trained groups initially from South Shore and Chatham. Neighborhood Voices was partially successful, and in fact reconfirmed how hard it was to create the tours that CAF had mastered. Most successful among

above: Each year Docent Appreciation Night celebrates the volunteer hours, new tours and notable achievements of CAF's dedicated docent corps. This 2007 gathering at the Intercontinental Hotel drew more than 300 docents. The Outstanding Docent Achievement Award, the highest honor given by the docent's peers each year, is the final surprise of the evening. (Photo: Anne Evans, CAF Archives)

opposite: As part of CAF's Neighborhood Voices program, Krisann Rehbein, manager of community partnerships and docent (back row, far right) and docent Tom Drebenstedt (front row, far right) collaborated with eager South Shore community groups in 2012. Residents trained and certified to give tours of their neighborhood. (Photo: Anne Evans, CAF Archives)

the communities was South Shore, where Prairie style houses, the Jackson Park Highlands (an area of stately early 20th-century architecture), the South Shore Cultural Center, Rainbow Beach and a nearby steel mill made tours of the area a joy for people to experience the city through its architecture.

The most elaborate "venturing out," and perhaps the most expansive CAF program ever, was what became known as Open House Chicago. This free annual festival was conceived after Lynn Osmond learned of the success of Open House London, a festival that began in 1992 and opened hundreds of buildings in London for a weekend. As the "Open House" concept had spread internationally, CAF sought funding to do the same in Chicago. "It was a free program, so it took time to raise the money," Osmond said. "So did convincing building owners that they could safely invite the public in." Board of trustees member John Pintozzi of Allstate Investments and chair of CAF's board finance committee was instrumental in garnering support from Allstate as Open House Chicago's first major donor. In later years, the James S. Kemper Foundation and Kemper Corporation became presenting sponsors.

In the first year of Open House Chicago, 2011, six neighborhoods and more than 100 buildings of interest opened their doors to the public. 23,000 people walked through to see places like Frank Lloyd Wright's Emil Bach House in Rogers Park and the Alfred Caldwell-designed gardens at Lake Point Tower. The next year, 13 neighborhoods and 150 buildings were involved from Uptown to Hyde Park, Humboldt Park to the Gold Coast and Little Village to the Loop. Helmut Jahn's presentation room in the rooftop cupola of the Jewelers Building along Wacker

Drive was open, as was the 1893 theater building in Pilsen, Thalia Hall, "an example of how a building serves communities as they change over time," said Bastiaan Bouma, CAF's first director of Open House Chicago. Staff and docents researched sites and served across the city by working with building managers, monitoring crowds and checking in with more than 1,100 volunteers. The observation deck of the Kemper Building, reopened after decades of being shuttered to the public, was the most popular spot during Open House Chicago's second year.

"Seeing hidden places, private spaces, widens the world for us," wrote *Chicago Tribune* columnist Mary Schmich in a column about Open House Chicago in 2014. CAF board of trustee chair John Pintozzi has called himself the number one fan of Open House Chicago. He made dozens of visits each of the years of the event. "It's a simple idea that addresses the organization's mission to show Chicago's variety through architecture," he said. "I find myself noticing details in places that I never really did before."

IMPACT BEYOND CHICAGO

As the Chicago Architecture Foundation grew and matured, it was a mark of satisfaction to find itself praised consistently in the national and international press. The *London Daily Telegraph* called its tours "superb." The *Washington Post* called the CAF River Cruise aboard Chicago's First Lady Cruises "one of the hotter tickets in town." So it was a not a shock, though perhaps a surprise, when Osmond received a call from Glen Murcutt, Pritzker Prize laureate in 2002. Murcutt modestly introduced himself as "an Australian architect" and told Lynn that he and a group in Sydney and Melbourne were discussing what would become the Australian Architecture Foundation.

2002-2011

Murcutt's objective, he said candidly, was to do what CAF had done so successfully with tours, exhibits and public engagement. Osmond said she was glad to help, and that led to an invitation to Australia to speak to organizers who would "promote contemporary architecture to as many people as possible," as the Australian Foundation soon stated as first among its aims. Murcutt and his colleagues believed that no one could provide advice on how to do it like Chicago could.

The growing importance of architecture in public discussion had the same effect elsewhere, as new centers for architecture were created in more than a dozen cities in this period. Of note, the Center of Architecture, an off-shoot of the local AIA New York chapter established in 2003, was a success from the start. They hosted hundreds of public events within a year of opening their storefront in lower Manhattan and rewriting the rules for how architectural professionals engage lay audiences. Dozens more AIA offices across the country quickly followed suit—efforts that met varying levels of success. But for almost all, CAF remained a beacon of sorts, working at a breadth and scale few could match.

Chicago's architectural culture was affirmed again when the Chicago Architecture Foundation and the American Architectural Foundation (AAF) linked forces in 2005 to undertake a project called the Architecture + Design Education Network (A+DEN). The board of regents at AAF had been searching for an opportunity to bolster national leadership in K-12 architecture education, an area where CAF had established roots. The two parties linked up to host a number of regional workshops and larger meetings, most held in Chicago. The American Institute of Architects' national office joined as a third partner the following year.

The continued delivery of new architecture centers, however, placed a larger calling on CAF, as inquiries for management counsel were received from organizations across the country. "Since 2003, the need had been identified for a central source and expert in the field to help other architecture centers develop and thrive," recalls Jan Grayson, CAF's board of trustees chair from 2001 to 2003. By 2009, the time came to officially launch the Association of Architecture Organizations (AAO), an independent entity with its own board of directors that could serve as an umbrella organization and information exchange for the many outfits around the U.S. with the common goal of enhancing public dialogue on architecture. A+DEN was reconfigured as a special interest group within AAO. And new interest groups were started for curators of architecture exhibitions, tour managers and the like. Osmond was indispensable to the new organization, which started hosting conferences throughout the country. By the end of its first five years of operation, AAO had expanded its network to encompass more than 160 members leading organizations in 70 U.S. cities and 10 other countries.

While the Chicago Architecture Foundation was proud to lead the way on many of these fronts, it quickly showed itself to be eager to learn from others as well. "What we do has always been about partnering with others," Osmond said. "Shared knowledge makes us all better at engaging the public with architecture."

Teaching youth at CAF through the iterative design process

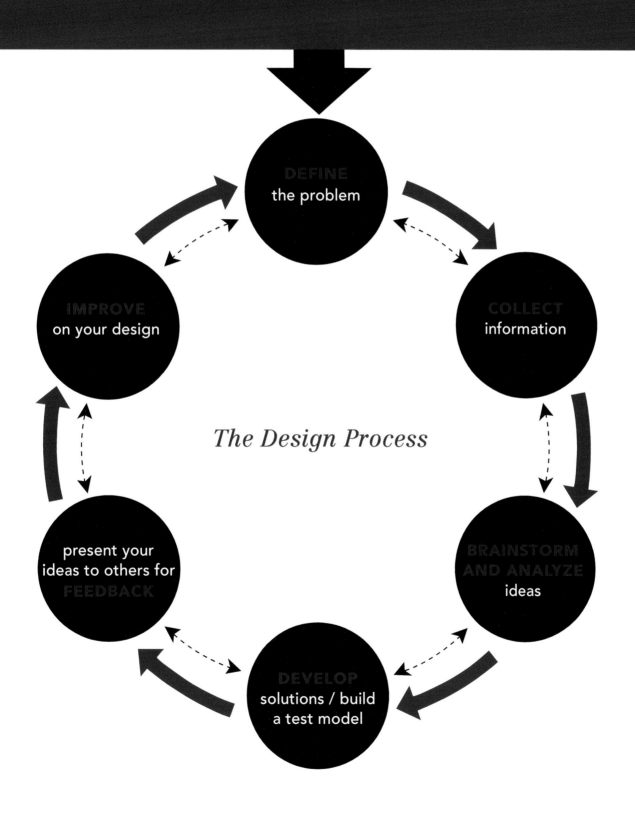

DEFINE
the problem

COLLECT
information

IMPROVE
on your design

The Design Process

present your
ideas to others for
FEEDBACK

BRAINSTORM
AND ANALYZE
ideas

DEVELOP
solutions / build
a test model

CHAPTER FIVE

A CENTER FOR DESIGN THINKING

2012 Mission statement: *The Chicago Architecture Foundation inspires people to discover why design matters.* CAF launches DiscoverDesign.org, a national digital platform connecting teens, teachers and architect mentors. CAF hosts 293,000 guests on tours. Open House Chicago attracts 40,000 visitors. *U.S. News and World Report* names CAF the "#1 best thing to do in Chicago." 2013 ArcelorMittal Design Studio @ CAF opens and LEGO® donates 500,000 white bricks. The AIA awards DiscoverDesign.org with a National Honor Award for Collaborative Achievement. Open House Chicago attracts 55,000 visitors. CAF partners with Skidmore, Owings & Merrill on *Great Cities, Great Lakes, Great Basin* exhibition. Visitor Experience Volunteer (VEV) program expands to serve visitors to CAF. Staff, volunteers and board of trustees members create CAF's first set of Core Values. 2014 Chicago's First Lady Cruises launches Chicago's Classic Lady. The American Architectural Foundation honors CAF with the Keystone Award. CAF opens *Chicago: City of Big Data* exhibition. Docents take more than 380,000 guests on tours. 2015 Docents launch a redesigned training program. CAF launches a completely redesigned architecture.org. TripAdvisor users rank the CAF River Cruise aboard Chicago's First Lady Cruises as the top tour in Chicago and one of the top 10 tours in America. CAF has 11,000 members and 212,000 social media followers. Inaugural Chicago Architecture Biennial opens at the Chicago Cultural Center, with CAF as the Official Education Partner. Open House Chicago attracts 85,000 visitors. CAF's *ChiDesign* competition draws 300 registrants from around the world to envision a new Center for Architecture, Design and Education (CADE). 2016 34th annual Newhouse Architecture and Design Competition. CAF has an annual audience of 650,000, a staff of 80 and a volunteer base of 2,000. CAF's new 2020 Strategic Plan lays the groundwork for a new permanent home, the Chicago Architecture Center. CAF and Glessner House Museum both celebrate their 50th anniversary on April 16.

By its 50th year, the Chicago Architecture Foundation was the seventh largest cultural institution in Chicago, quite a distinction in a city well-known for its museums. In some ways CAF appeared to be a traditional cultural institution, with tours, exhibits and well-regarded speakers attracting a curious public. But in other ways it was different. It was still largely the "invisible museum," a reference to its status as a museum largely without walls. Yet its impact on the city was conspicuous and growing steadily.

Important benchmarks showed CAF's growth. In 2014, the Agra family introduced their fourth vessel in the fleet for the CAF River Cruise aboard Chicago's First Lady Cruises. The christening of Chicago's Classic Lady was a milestone not just for CAF but for Chicago at large. The city was promoting itself as a destination as never before and benefiting from the wave of architectural tourism.

It was particularly gratifying that in 2012, *U.S. News and World Report* named CAF the "#1 best thing to do in Chicago." In 2015, TripAdvisor users ranked the CAF River Cruise the top tour in Chicago and "one of the top 10 tours" in America—a result of CAF's unmatched docents who not only met the rising demand for tours but continued their vital role in the organization as educators and passionate advocates for architecture and design. "Despite increased competition across Chicago, our tour attendance nearly doubled in the last six years," said Michael Malak, vice president of operations and business strategy, who fostered growth in both tours and retail at CAF. In 2015, the organization had an annual attendance of 643,000 people and an operating budget of $20 million.

top to bottom:
Since partnering in 1993, CAF and Chicago's First Lady Cruises watched interest in the River Cruise skyrocket. The first boats were not big enough to meet public demand. As a result, Chicago's First Lady Cruises launched Chicago's Fair Lady in 2006, Chicago's Leading Lady in 2011, followed by Chicago's Classic Lady in 2014. (Photo, left: Anne Evans, CAF Archives) (Photo, right: Courtesy Chicago's First Lady Cruises)

CAF's partnership with the Museum of Contemporary Art (MCA) on a new series called "Architecture is Art" brought renowned architects and artists together for conversation around the intersection of their two disciplines. In 2013, Reed Kroloff, CAF's Senior Advisor for Programs and Industry Collaboration interviewed Jaume Plensa, the Catalan artist who created the Crown Fountain in Millennium Park. (Photo: Anne Evans, CAF Archives)

Another area of growth was the Open House Chicago festival. In 2015, more than 85,000 people participated in this two day event. During the first five years of Open House, approximately 280,000 attendees made more than one million visits to buildings and sites in and around the city. Through their patronage of local restaurants and businesses, attendees collectively contributed $25.4 million to the Chicago economy between 2011 and 2015. The focus of the festival remained neighborhood exploration and the creation of community. Open House Chicago encouraged people to visit parts of the city that were unfamiliar to them. Residents from South Shore were visiting Lincoln Park, and residents from Edgewater were visiting North Lawndale. As hundreds of thousands of people experienced the cultures of neighborhoods that were often misrepresented in the media, new

right, top to bottom:
In 2015, Open House Chicago visitors explored the newly-restored Chicago Athletic Association Hotel along Michigan Avenue. (Photo: Glenn Kaupert, CAF Archives)

By 2015, Open House Chicago had more than 1,600 volunteers stationed at sites across the city. These volunteers enthusiastically greeted visitors, answered questions and tracked attendance on behalf of CAF. For many volunteers it was a chance to see a neighborhood they may not have previously visited. (Photo: Anne Evans, CAF Archives)

above: In 2014 Open House Chicago advertised on bus shelters, as well as CTA buses and trains. The campaign invited visitors to explore the hidden gems and architectural treasures of Chicago's diverse neighborhoods—all for free. (Photo: Anne Evans, CAF Archives)

perceptions began to emerge. In studies conducted during the first five years of Open House, more than 200,000 people indicated that they had improved perceptions of Chicago's neighborhoods as a result of the event. By 2015, Open House Chicago was one of the largest architecture events in the world.

EXPANDING THE DEFINITION OF ARCHITECTURE THROUGH EXHIBITS

Popular success was matched by creative triumphs, as CAF was mounting exhibits in the atrium gallery that pushed the envelope in terms of content and presentation. While exhibitions still focused on the role of design in the built environment, some subjects were crossing into areas that might have seemed beyond the scope of "architecture" not too many years before. Exhibits touched on politics, technology, planning and other topics. They often addressed the built environment with a scope that spanned regions and crossed national borders.

Of the latter category was *Great Cities, Great Lakes, Great Basin,* organized in a 2014 partnership with Skidmore, Owings & Merrill (SOM), which showed that decisions made anywhere on the five lakes, including two countries and dozens of cities, are closely interconnected. The undeniable argument was that water quality, suburban sprawl, transportation and other issues required collective, not splintered, action. The exhibit addressed "an awareness challenge that we are all part of this unique watershed," said Phil Enquist, partner at SOM which had studied the question for several years and contributed its powerful content.

Great Cities, Great Lakes, Great Basin had modern thinking and logic, but its maps, pictures and text were made more powerful by something that might not have been expected when the exhibit was conceived—the *Chicago Model* still dominated the atrium gallery. Striking exhibit panels, designed by Rick Valicenti of Thirst, a communication design practice, told of problems and opportunities all around the Great Lakes. The model in the middle showed a city of enormous impact on anything that it touched.

right: CAF's 2014 exhibition, *Great Cities, Great Lakes, Great Basin*—centered around the city model—was organized in partnership with Skidmore Owings & Merrill and the International Secretariat for Water, based in Montreal. It presented a 100-year vision to guide the planning and development in the international watershed of the Great Lakes. (Photo: Courtesy SOM)

2012-2016

Exhibits with big ideas became regular events at CAF. From 2007 to 2013, exhibits were led by Greg Dreicer as vice president of interpretation and exhibitions. Dreicer had developed numerous exhibits that explored the intersection of the humanities and technology. Much of his scholarly work examined the complex forces that underline buildings and cities—the idea that architecture represents a process driven by human decisions and behavior, technology and ideas.

Dreicer's projects addressed a range of subjects from preservation to sustainability, and the last exhibit that he conceived before leaving Chicago may have been CAF's most audacious. *Chicago: City of Big Data* revealed the increasingly important impact that the velocity, variety and volume of digital data had on design decisions in cities. The exhibition, using the Chicago model as its centerpiece, was developed and executed by curator Ingrid Haftel who skillfully made the complex topic relevant and accessible to the general public. The exhibition showed that design decisions could be, and often were, guided by oceans of data points—from social media feeds to surveillance cameras.

The idea made intuitive sense to anyone interested in urban design, but it was still abstract and involved a plethora of sources of information. So it required collaborators, which played neatly into one of CAF's longtime strengths. "Partnerships allows us to punch above our weight," said Lynn Osmond as she encouraged the ambitious project. Partners arrived from the city government, universities and private business. They were drawn to the project by the atrium venue and by CAF's longtime ability to bring in participants from many fields.

"Data represents an unseen architecture," said John Tolva, who was then chief technology officer for the City of Chicago and a member of the CAF board of trustees. The exhibit represented a collaboration opportunity for Tolva, who had long been dedicated to helping cities use information technology to improve decision making. In the exhibit, the invisible data of the city became intensely visible with an overhead projection system that layered colors on buildings, streets and neighborhoods of the expansive city model. The colors illustrated information such as transportation data, Chicago's call center requests and energy consumption. The exhibition also explained that data-driven cities are nothing new, that Chicago's early planners also collected and parsed statistics. "We used the exhibit as a catalyzing factor in how we discussed data and its role in planning today," said Brenna Berman, chief information officer for the City of Chicago. "The exhibit was a great touchpoint."

THE TRAVEL PROGRAM

As exhibitions expanded CAF's scope, so too did travel to other cities and countries. Each year, beginning in the 1990s, CAF staff planned trips for donors and members to view architecture in other cities—somewhat modeled on the regional enrichment trips that docents had been taking for years. The first international members' trip to London set the standard for CAF travel for some time to come. A Berlin trip was offered the following year. Singapore and Kuala Lumpur came later. There was nothing commonplace about these tours, even those within the U.S., in part because donor and docent Barry Sears (class of 1992) scouted locations prior to each trip and made the arrival of Chicagoans nearly as much of an event for the hosts as for the visitors.

opposite: Chicago: City of Big Data was CAF's second exhibition of 2014. It explored the increasingly complex connections between people, information and data. The exhibition showed how voluminous data, collected and interpreted, could be used by citizens and civic leaders alike to broaden understanding of the city and shape urban design decisions. In the exhibit, lights of various colors were projected on the city model to help visualize Chicago's diverse public data sets such as landmarks, potholes and energy use. (Photo: Anne Evans, CAF Archives)

And like so many CAF activities, the trips were available almost nowhere else and featured serious architectural intent. In 2016, a CAF group of 25 people traveled to Havana shortly after the United States normalized diplomatic relations with Cuba. The trip was timely, said CAF founding board member Dirk Lohan, who was on the tour. Lohan thought it was important to go to Cuba before commercial forces kicked in again and changed the island's character.

GOING DIGITAL

In the 2010s, CAF's expansion began to reach deeply into the digital realm. But CAF's digital presence actually began as early as 1995 when CAF store employee Kelly Jones suggested that the organization start an official website. Leadership at the time balked, questioning if such an expense was needed. Jones was convinced, however, and he took it upon himself to reserve the address "architecture.org" for CAF. He told management what he had done. They were still unimpressed, and so Jones himself paid the maintenance costs for the URL for several years. Under director of operations Sally Hess, Jones quietly worked with a web developer to create CAF's first online presence with an internet address that has been invaluable in staking CAF's claim on architectural interpretation.

It was typical of CAF that one of the more effective efforts in digital marketing began spontaneously, or "organically," as its instigator Jennifer Lucente (later McElroy) put it. Lucente had been hired in the marketing department in 2008 to manage mailing lists and otherwise work on traditional campaigns. But she also knew that social media represented a huge opportunity, so largely on her own, she set up CAF on Facebook, Twitter and other social media platforms. It became obvious almost immediately that social media could expand CAF's relationships among people who knew little about the organization.

Then in 2010, Lucente went a step further, announcing that she was about to embark on something called the "85 Tours Challenge." As if it were a round-the-world adventure, she would take each of the CAF's 85 tours in one

above, left to right:
During the 2016 Member Travel Program, founding board of trustees member Dirk Lohan, chatted with the director of the National Arts Center in Havana during a tour of the campus, designed in the early 1960s by Cuban architect Ricardo Porro. Lohan was one of 25 CAF members to explore the capital city with CAF shortly after the United States normalized diplomatic relations with Cuba. (Photo: Courtesy CAF docent Delta Green)

In 2013, CAF members visited architectural landmarks in and around Pittsburgh, including Fallingwater, Frank Lloyd Wright's 1930s masterpiece. (Photo: Vincent Chung, CAF Archives)

opposite: CAF staff member Jennifer Lucente recognized the growing power of social media and imagined a new marketing campaign using these digital platforms. In 2010 she organized and publicized her personal odyssey in taking all 85 of CAF's tours. As she shared her experiences, CAF gained hundreds of followers, many of whom celebrated Lucente's final tour in December at the Chicago Theater. (Photo: Anne Evans, CAF Archives)

year and share her experiences on social media. People, many of whom had never been on a CAF tour themselves, took notice and joined her on this journey. Lucente even met her future husband when he joined her on a tour of Frank Lloyd Wright houses in Oak Park.

Gradually but not too surprisingly, CAF began to attract young, digitally-savvy staff, for whom the potential of digital outreach seemed both ordinary and limitless. "We knew we had to make a digital leap forward," said Jill Farley, who began as a web specialist charged with updating architecture.org and other online properties. Within a couple of years, Farley became director of digital initiatives and pushed for a new set of objectives. CAF needed a website that didn't just promote tours and event registrations. The organization wanted architecture.org to be interactive, full of unique content and a visually-rich resource for people with an interest in architecture and history.

By 2013, CAF developed a digital strategy alongside a marketing firm called IA Collaborative, and not surprisingly it overlapped with the organization's overall mission and role. The digital strategy's guiding principles were familiar: to "humanize" architecture; to "refresh people's view" of Chicago; to serve as a forum for "civic issues" for Chicagoans; and to "orient" tourists and locals alike as they explored the built environment. In 2015, CAF launched a completely new architecture.org designed by Fastspot, a Baltimore firm. It was as much a source of architectural information, with articles and videos, as it was a marketing tool. Within CAF, the team responsible for the new website included Farley, as well as web developer Tushar Samant, director of marketing operations and docent Patrick Miner (class of 2012), digital strategist and docent Molly Page (class of 2013), web specialist Ashley Powers and vice president of marketing Marilyn Jackson. By 2016, Jackson would call the digital presence of the organization "holistic." Filled with authoritative information about the built environment, architecture.org also had a user-friendly feel that CAF modeled on the enthusiastic personalities of the docent corps.

right: In 1995 CAF acquired the coveted URL "architecture.org." By the 21st century the organization recognized the need for a website that did more than promote tours and events. After a year-long digital strategy project, CAF launched a completely redesigned website in 2015 which included a wealth of content and images to tell Chicago's architectural stories.
(Photo: Courtesy Fastspot)

A significant portion of CAF's growth in membership and overall audience in the 2010s was the result of experiments in digital engagement. By 2015 CAF had 11,000 members and 212,000 social media followers. There were some remarkable stories along the way. When Instagram rose in popularity from 2010 to 2015, it was particularly powerful, said Molly Page who was managing CAF's Instagram account. Often she posted pictures of buildings with little commentary, instead choosing to elicit the curiosity of followers. "It was always great to see why others were interested in a building, like how someone's grandfather had worked on it a long time ago," Page said.

TEACHING DESIGN AS A PROCESS

Social media and communication with a wider general audience was not the only way that CAF was impacted by new digital capabilities. With the success of *The Architecture Handbook: A Student Guide to Understanding Buildings*, CAF's high school textbook published in 2007, the education team embarked on a new challenge. Using digital tools familiar to students, CAF sought to radically change the way that teens learn about the design process. CAF and the design community also recognized it was critical for students to have opportunities to creatively solve design problems that mattered to them. Over a three-year period culminating in a 2012 launch, CAF staff Jen Masengarb, Krisann Rehbein and Jill Farley—with digital strategy help from board of trustees member John Tolva—brought together more than 150 architects, educators and teens from 14 high schools to create an innovative digital learning tool. Students in Chicago Public Schools and suburban Chicago, as well as in Alaska, Florida, California and New Jersey provided valuable feedback over a year of pilot testing.

On DiscoverDesign.org, students chose real-world design challenges posted online by CAF and then worked through the iterative steps of the design process (i.e. define the problem, collect information, brainstorm ideas, develop a solution, get feedback and present a final design). In solving challenges such as redesigning school lockers, libraries or cafeterias, students posted their photos, digital models, animations, videos, drawings and text then received feedback from their peers, their teachers and from design professionals across the country who were volunteering as online mentors. CAF soon began using DiscoverDesign.org to host an annual national competition that paralleled its successful Newhouse Competition for local students. By 2015, more than 7,300 users had joined the website.

THE DESIGN STUDIO

The Chicago Architecture Foundation was behaving like a major museum in many ways as it approached 50 years of age. Through increasingly detailed audience research, led by Marilyn Jackson, CAF began to better understand its current and potential audiences. This led to various programming decisions, including the creation of the Design Studio which, in 2013, replaced the CitySpace gallery off the Jackson Boulevard entrance of the Railway Exchange building. Here the public could experience architecture in a hands-on way.

"We brainstormed about the Design Studio," said Elory Rozner, an independent educational consultant who worked with staff on the project. "For one, we needed

opposite top: DiscoverDesign.org, CAF's unique digital platform introduced teens to the design process. The site was launched in 2012 as an educational tool, with design challenges and social networking features connecting high schoolers across the country with their peers, their teachers and architects volunteering as mentors for project-based learning in architecture. (Photo: CAF Archives)

opposite middle, left to right:
The city model became a focal point of CAF field trips departing from the Railway Exchange Building. Docents commonly used the model to orient students to Chicago's geography, scale and growth. (Photo: Anne Evans, CAF Archives)

Tocarra Mallard, Manager of Studio Programs, worked with families during "Read and Build," CAF's series for young children (ages 3-5). Each month children worked on art projects and listened to stories that explored the building blocks of architecture and the city. (Photo: Jesse Banwart, CAF Archives)

opposite bottom: CAF's annual Engineering Fest, celebrated each February, provided opportunities for children and families to build models, take tours, learn about careers and enjoy working together to solve design challenges. In 2016, more than 1,300 people attended the 2-day event at CAF. (Photo: Anne Evans, CAF Archives)

above: Building with LEGO® became one of the most popular and visually-striking activities in The ArcelorMittal Design Studio. More than 500,000 LEGO® bricks were generously donated to CAF by the LEGO Group. (Photo: Anne Evans, CAF Archives)

a place where people could spread projects out and make a mess." That meant students of all ages, children and adults, were invited to use the space to design and draw as architects did. The Design Studio became a place where architects worked with high school students, where CAF staff worked with teachers, and where families could learn about how cities are built.

"We Are All Designers" was emblazoned on the wall to promote the concept of design thinking—an iterative process used to creatively solve a problem. On a nationwide basis, this was the concept behind STEM education initiatives, where science, technology, engineering and math became increasingly stressed in schools. CAF was now seeing itself as a key participant in the movement. "We measure our success in how well we teach design as the solution to real-world problems," said Gabrielle Lyon, vice president of education and experience. Lyon's work transformed and deepened the ways in which CAF engaged youth and adults in the design process while also building the organization's capacity to serve larger numbers of learners.

With design thinking in mind, the involvement of steel giant ArcelorMittal as the primary sponsor of the Design Studio went well beyond making its name known to the public. The Design Studio was teaching concepts that future employees at companies would need to know, according to Bill Steers, corporate responsibility executive at ArcelorMittal. "The Design Studio opens people's eyes more broadly about how design works," he said. "It expands people's imaginations about the built environment and how they might contribute to it in the future."

After the launch of the ArcelorMittal Design Studio, the space became the home for a number of new education programs, including CAF's first-ever summer camps, a new Teen Academy with a multi-year fellows program and collaborative evening programs with nearby nonprofit After School Matters (ASM). One of the most popular and visually striking activities in the ArcelorMittal Design Studio was building with LEGO®. Both children and adults enjoyed creating with the all-white LEGO® "architecture studio" bricks. Vice president of institutional advancement Jennifer Van Valkenburg worked to secure a generous donation from the LEGO Group. When she received a call from the Railway Exchange building loading dock one afternoon, Van Valkenburg discovered the immensity of their donation. Packed in boxes on pallets stood 500,000 LEGO® bricks awaiting a child's limitless imagination.

The Design Studio was just one initiative considered by the Washington-based American Architectural Foundation when it honored CAF with its Keystone Award in 2014. Youth education and engaging docent-led tours were cited as programs that merited this prestigious award for "exemplary design leadership that improves lives and transforms communities." Past recipients included the Museum of Modern Art (MOMA), Former Secretary of State Hillary Clinton and Mayor Richard M. Daley. This "signified that we are making a profound impact globally to inspire people to discover why design matters," said Lynn Osmond in accepting the award. It also showed how the architectural profession considered outreach to the public a key component in the future of architecture.

A CULTURE OF VOLUNTEER EXCELLENCE

As CAF has evolved, many milestones have been achieved through shared goals and organic growth. But as the organization's profile rose, and as the public's demand for architectural knowledge increased, intensive and long-term planning became necessary on every level of CAF. A 2016 Strategic Advancement Plan, completed in 2012, pushed to strengthen several characteristics of the organization. Docent Jill Tanz (class of 2003, docent council president from 2009 to 2011 and later a board of trustees member) encouraged the council to hold a retreat in order to look for ways that the docent corps might further the strategic plan. One of the plan's eight goals was to "build a strong, aligned team." It resonated with the docents and incoming docent council president Mary Jo Hoag (class of 2007 and council president from 2012 to 2014). Docent Mike Cohen (class of 1998) and the council led an effort to codify the core characteristics of CAF's unique docent culture—unlike almost any other cultural organization in the country. The docent corps' self-governed training, policies and peer review were rooted in a supportive training program. A collegial environment of teaching and learning valued docent individuality and freedom of expression in the creation and delivery of tours.

Out of this docent council retreat grew the need to reexamine the entire docent program, not just the training. Docents looked for ways to increase the capacity and readiness of their peers to adapt to changing audience needs, deepen their knowledge and skillsets and continue to retain a diverse, committed and excellent docent corps. Docent Jane Buckwalter (class of 1998 and council president from 2001 to 2003) and Barbara Gordon, vice president of program operations and a docent (class of 1995), chaired a year-long process that brought together 37 docents and seven staff on six ad-hoc committees (training, rapid response, recruitment and selection, service and commitment, policy and transition).

Launched in 2015, a redesigned docent program now included a new three-part training model. The model, designed by the training ad hoc committee chaired by docent Delta Green (class of 2008) included an orientation to CAF and a five-week module on the "Fundamentals of Chicago Architecture" that expanded beyond

opposite top: Jen Masengarb, director of interpretation and research, worked with all ages and audience groups at CAF, including these teens at a 2015 summer camp. Here along Dearborn Street, the teens were introduced to Chicago's early skyscrapers, such as the 1891 Monadnock Building. (Photo: Jesse Banwart, CAF Archives)

opposite middle, left to right:
To cultivate the next generation of design-thinkers and -doers, CAF created a Teen Academy program. Through workshops, after school and summer programs, competitions, multi-year cohorts and internships, CAF teens learned new design skills. (Photo: Manny Juarez, CAF Archives)

The Teen Academy also included hard-hat tours, introducing teens to various career pathways in architecture, engineering, construction and design. (Photo: Jesse Banwart, CAF Archives)

opposite bottom: In 2014, the American Architectural Foundation (AAF) honored CAF with its prestigious Keystone Award. AAF President Ron Bogle (far left) and AAF Executive Committee Chair G. Sandy Diehl (far right) presented the award to Lynn Osmond, President and CEO (center right) who was joined by former board of trustees chairs John Syvertsen, Walt Eckenhoff (second and third from left) and John Pintozzi (second from right). (Photo: Courtesy American Architectural Foundation)

Loop skyscrapers and taught concepts through a series of 10 case study buildings from across the city. It concluded with four or five-week modules to teach tours that needed additional docents. Docent Donna Gabanski (class of 1994 and council president from 2003 to 2005) who chaired the training subcommittee of the education committee since 2005 remarked, "The new training format was modeled after a university degree path where docents receive a common base of information that remains consistent each year, before moving on to 'major' in a specific tour." This scholarly and practical course, akin to a graduate-level seminar, became more focused and intentional for the trainees. The new course included weekly lectures given by outside experts, docents and staff, as well as readings, reading discussions with staff, written homework, explorations of the city, hands-on activities and training in storytelling strategies. Unchanged in the entire process was the peer-to-peer learning environment. Staff facilitated a complex system where each trainee was assigned three experienced docents to serve as their homework reader, sponsor and tour certifier.

Another outgrowth of the Strategic Plan was a new "rapid response" committee of docents and staff created to react quickly to new opportunities and requests from potential partners. For example, docents wrote a new Navy Pier tour when a redesign for that landmark was announced. The docents also created tours for the American Institute of Architects when Chicago hosted its annual convention.

One hurdle for the organization had always been to assist visitors at CAF and increase their awareness of CAF's many offerings. This became another volunteer opportunity, and it was filled by a group called Visitor Experience Volunteers (VEVs). What became the VEV program first began in 2002 when the CitySpace Gallery drew people in off the street. Exhibition panels and a small model of the city elicited questions, and volunteers came on to handle answers and engage curious individuals.

By 2013, Hallie Rosen, director of volunteer engagement and a docent (class of 2010), moved to expand this volunteer corps. She stationed VEVs to answer questions about tours and exhibits, to take tickets and to assemble tour groups. The program, which involved nearly 100 VEVs after several years, became enriching for volunteers and visitors alike. Among the first VEVs was Harry Eisenman, a former history of technology professor from Missouri who moved to Chicago because he and his wife wanted to retire to a large walkable city. "We meet people from all over the world," he said, "and we learn so much about what interests them about Chicago." He learned that the CAF River Cruise, Frank Lloyd Wright and ornamental historic buildings were always high on the list. By seeking to understand the visitor's curiosity, and with all CAF had to offer, VEVs like Eisenman became an indispensable link.

In the midst of all these changes, volunteers and staff alike felt that there was a need to augment the 2016 strategic plan with a statement of CAF's core values— distilled and written primarily by a working group of staff, volunteers and board members. It was a cogent and heartfelt list, including an overarching sense of collaboration, commitment to lifelong learning, patient respect for visitors and colleagues and high level of integrity. These core values guided CAF's continued growth as it had evolved for a half century before.

opposite, top to bottom:
CAF's docents furthered their dedication to excellence when they redesigned the training program throughout 2014, largely to enable the diverse and committed corps to more quickly adapt to new opportunities. New docents proudly earned their CAF badge after graduating from the program, just as the first docent class did in 1971. Here, docent Tom Carmichael discusses the Marquette Building lobby. (Photo: Anne Evans, CAF Archives)

Docent-led tours of Millennium Park became some of the most popular in CAF's catalogue. Here a docent stops to highlight the *Cloud Gate* sculpture (affectionately known in as "The Bean") designed by artist Anish Kapoor. (Photo: Anne Evans, CAF Archives)

top to bottom:

The "Sculpture in the Loop" tour explored how artists and architects collaborate in creating successful works of public art. Docent Deb Rodak discussed the Chicago *Picasso* in Daley Plaza. Other highlights include stops in Federal Plaza (Calder's *Flamingo*) and Chase Plaza (Chagall's *Four Seasons*). (Photo: Anne Evans, CAF Archives)

Docent and docent council president Ellen Shubart led the "Elevated Architecture" tour which offered visitors to the Loop a unique architectural perspective of the city at several different L stops. (Photo: Anne Evans, CAF archives)

On one of CAF's pedway walking tours, docent Kenton Foutty stopped at Chicago City Hall/County Building to discuss the building's history. The pedway tours, using tunnels which link buildings throughout the Loop, became very popular in winter. Visitors had the chance to experience the "city under the city." (Photo: Anne Evans, CAF Archives)

"The better informed Chicagoans are about their communities and why design matters, the more they will advocate for the highest standards in architecture and urban design."

LYNN OSMOND, HON. AIA, PRESIDENT AND CEO, CHICAGO ARCHITECTURE FOUNDATION
2016

©Dot Ward/BP America

left to right:
At the inaugural Chicago Architecture Biennial in 2015, Teen Ambassadors were trained by CAF to help the public better understand several of the event's major installations. As the Biennial's Signature Education Partner, CAF selected and trained 15 local teens who interacted each weekend with visitors at Biennial venues at the Cultural Center. (Photo: Jen Masengarb, CAF Archives)

Chicago Mayor Rahm Emanuel (second row, center), Co-Artistic Director of the Chicago Architecture Biennial Sarah Herda (back row, second from right), and CAF President and CEO Lynn Osmond (back row, center) were among the dignitaries who celebrated with the student winners of the BP Student Design Competition. The competition, organized and run by CAF as part of the Biennial, challenged CPS high school students to design "pocket parks" designed to improve access to public open space. (Photo: courtesy Dot Ward, BP America)

opposite: With its 2015 *ChiDesign* competition, CAF's Board of Trustees invited designers to consider what a future home for CAF could look like. The design brief called for a "Center for Architecture, Design and Education" and drew visionary responses from architects around the world. Submissions were not intended to be final designs, rather a basis for ideas, partnerships and support needed to make the Center a reality. (Photo: Jonathan Loïc Rogers, CAF Archives)

READY FOR A NEW ERA

CAF's footprint had grown steadily since its founding, and by the 21st century it had become a strong voice in the field of architecture and design nationwide. This was evident with the 2015 Chicago Architecture Biennial, North America's largest international survey of contemporary architecture. Its installations that explored "The State of the Art of Architecture" provided a snapshot of the ways more than 100 designers in 30 countries wrestled with the day's most pressing global issues.

CAF participated as "signature education partner" in the Biennial and hosted several programs, most to promote design-thinking for young people. CAF trained 15 local teens—recruited and paid through After School Matters—to become "Biennial Ambassadors" who over 12 weekends of the event would guide and engage Biennial visitors from around the world. Another student program, the BP Design Competition, had high school students design "pocket parks" on small footprints, even vacant lots, in neighborhoods around Chicago. Also coinciding with the Biennial, CAF hosted *Currencies of Architecture*, an exhibition mounted by the Chicago Architectural Club. In the exhibit, architect Stanley Tigerman unveiled a 21st-century image meant to reexamine and update his iconic 1978 collage called "The Titanic," which came to represent the end of modernism.

CAF's most far-reaching exhibit for the Biennial was experimental in nature but inspired by a realistic objective. The *ChiDesign* competition, which drew nearly 300 registrants from around the world, asked designers to envision a new Center for Architecture, Design and Education (CADE) in Chicago. *ChiDesign* was based on the idea that CAF would someday have its own building. "We need to more fully occupy our name," said John Syvertsen, CAF board of trustees chair from 2005 to 2008 and a CAF docent (class of 2016). Syvertsen and Walt Eckenhoff, chair from 2003 to 2005, had been key figures in the *ChiDesign* competition and the concept development of the Architecture Center.

The *ChiDesign* competition brief called for a building with a variety of uses, including a "design and allied arts high school." Entries included space for CAF's offices, galleries and workshops. Also envisioned were offices for the

Council on Tall Buildings and Urban Habitat (CTBUH) and room for numerous educational activities planned for the Center. The competition was facilitated by CAF consultant and senior program advisor Reed Kroloff and juried by Stanley Tigerman, David Adjaye, Ned Cramer, Billie Tsien and Monica Ponce de Leon. The jury named five winners and several dozen entries were displayed in the CAF atrium gallery surrounding the *Chicago Model.*

THE FUTURE OF THE CHICAGO ARCHITECTURE FOUNDATION

On April 16, 2016, the Chicago Architecture Foundation turned 50 years old. The organization is now at a pivotal moment in its history. With an annual audience of 650,000, a staff of 80 and a volunteer base of nearly 2,000, CAF is one of Chicago's 10 largest cultural institutions, but is the only one without a permanent home. CAF's comprehensive 2020 strategic plan lays the groundwork for a monumental evolution of the organization. The plan calls for expanded STEM-based educational opportunities for young people; further development of programs to connect the public with key issues facing the urban environment; greater public engagement to encourage Chicagoans to influence the design of their communities; and the strengthening of CAF's role as a cultural ambassador for Chicago.

After years of incredible growth, CAF has reached the limits of its current rental space at the Railway Exchange Building. As the organization has expanded, it has cobbled together spaces, eventually occupying 20,000 square feet scattered throughout this office building. The space serves hundreds of thousands of guests who visit CAF for tours, exhibitions, programs and education. But the lack of ample classroom spaces makes it especially difficult for CAF to expand its education programs, a key goal in the strategic plan. The fact that the world's largest architecture organization does not have a permanent, purpose-built facility limits CAF's ability to expand.

As part of its 50th anniversary celebration, CAF is announcing that it will develop a new permanent home, the Chicago Architecture Center. The Center will be centrally located in the Loop, close to the Chicago River and Millennium Park. Under the leadership of board of trustees chair John Pintozzi, committee chair Walt Eckenhoff and President and CEO Lynn Osmond, CAF envisions a new Center that will provide a venue for design education to flourish. It will be a place for the public to engage in new and meaningful ways with the built environment and with the story of architectural innovation in Chicago. Plans for the Center include an expanded *Chicago Model* as well as exhibitions on skyscrapers and Chicago's influential architects. The new Center will include a dedicated design education facility that will be a resource for Chicagoans to learn about and discuss their city's future. The building will continue CAF's legacy for many years to come by serving as a place for docents to begin and end their tours.

By creating a new Center, CAF aims to affirm the critical role that architecture and design play in Chicago's future. As part of a larger design campus, the Center will also include other educational and design-affiliated organizations. It will be the nation's leading education center for training the next generation of designers and problem solvers.

The Center will become the focal point for Chicagoans to meet, debate and discuss what the city's next 50 years should look like. It will welcome the world to the doorstep of architectural innovation and lead the way into the future. Daniel Burnham famously said, "make no little plans," and this statement captures CAF's bold vision. CAF is "making big plans, aiming high in hope and work," because Chicago deserves a place to showcase its great architecture and the impact its architects continue to have on the world. Building on the accomplishments of its first 50 years, CAF will create the Chicago Architecture Center, a place where people of all ages can come together. A place where millions of people can witness and participate in the immense power of design to improve lives. Where people can look up and say, "this is why design matters."

Social media engagement shows scale of Open House Chicago

In the first five years of Open House Chicago

- *1 million+* **site visits**

- *280,000* **attendees**

- *440+* **buildings**

- *$25.4 million* **economic impact**

- *200,000* **people have improved** *perceptions of Chicago neighborhoods because of Open House Chicago*

Photos: CAF Archives, Anne Evans, Eric Allix Rogers, Pete Hill and Razvan Sera

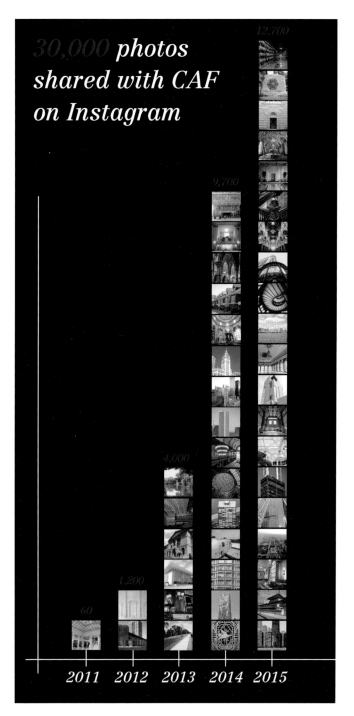

30,000 *photos shared with CAF on Instagram*

12,700

9,700

4,000

1,200

60

2011 2012 2013 2014 2015

Early Board meeting for the Chicago School of Architecture Foundation in the Glessner House library. August 1966 (Photo: Richard Nickel, CAF Archives)

BOARD PRESIDENTS AND CHAIRS

1966
Richard Wintergreen

1967–1969
Wilbert Hasbrouck, Ben Weese

1970–1971
Ben Weese, Marian Despres

1972
Ralph Youngren, Marian Despres

1973
Ralph Youngren, Marian Despres

1974
Ralph Youngren, James Nagle,
Marian Despres

1975
James Nagle, Richard DuBrul,
Marian Despres

1976
Martha Vanderwicken,
Marian Despres

1977
Marian Despres

1978–1979
Ruth Moore Garbe

1979–1981
Franklin Orwin

1981–1983
John Montgomery III

1983–1986
Robert A. Hutchins

1986–1988
Thomas Samuels

1988–1990
Grant McCullagh

1990–1993
Henry Kuehn

1993–1994
Jeffrey Jahns

1994–1995
Ted Peterson

1995–1999
David Hart

1999–2001
Dan Maguire

2001–2003
Jan Grayson

2003–2005
Walt Eckenhoff

2005–2008
John Syvertsen

2008–2010
John DiCiurcio

2010–2012
Steven G.M. Stein

2012–
John Pintozzi

Chicago Architecture Foundation Board of Trustees. December 2015 (Photo: CAF)

DOCENT COUNCIL PRESIDENTS

Ex-Officio Members

Ryan Biziorek
  Associate, Arup
Delta Greene
  Docent at Large
Scott Rappe
  Principal, Kuklinski + Pappe
Ellen Shubart
  Docent Council President

Life Trustee

Henry H. Kuehn

Trustees Emeritus

John DiCiurcio
  CEO, Flatiron Construction
Jan Grayson
  Managing Partner,
  JMG & Associates
Jeffrey Jahns
  Partner, Seyfarth Shaw
Daniel Maguire
  Chief Executive Officer (Retired),
  Executive Construction Inc.
Lloyd B. Morgan
  Morgan Interests, LLC
Richard H. Schnadig
  Special Assistant Corporation
  Counsel, City of Chicago
  Department of Law
Wilmont "Vic" Vickrey
  Founding Principal,
  VOA Associates Incorporated
John J. Viera
  Commonwealth Edison (Retired)

1971–1972
John Thorpe

1972–1973
Bill Burgess

1974–1975
Cynthia Parry

1976–1977
Nancy Glassberg

1977–1979
Henry Klein

1979–1981
Ken Monroe

1981–1983
Joe La Rue

1983
Pat Sparks

1984
Karen Bronzyski

1985–1986
Bill Hoffman

1987–1988
Phyllis Kozlowski

1988
Dick Spurgin

1988–1990
Dan Fitzgerald

1990
Ken Monroe

1991
Mary Lou Caldwell

1992
Mike Weiland

1993–1994
Tom Drebenstedt

1995
Arlene Hausman

1996–1999
Tori Simms

1999–2001
Judith Randall

2001–2003
Jane Buckwalter

2003–2005
Donna Gabanski

2005–2007
Bobbi Pinkert

2007–2009
Charles Stanford

2009–2011
Jill Tanz

2011–2014
Mary Jo Hoag

2014–
Ellen Shubart

Elected Members

Emily Clott
Class of 2012

Georgia Goldberg
Class of 2012

Delta Green
Class of 2008

Harry Hirsch
Class of 1998

Judith Kaufman
Class of 2010

Bill Lipsman
Class of 2009

Bobbi Pinkert
Class of 1999

Constance Rajala
Class of 2008

Cindy Schneider
Class of 2010

Ellen Shubart, President
Class of 2006

Leanne Star
Class of 2011

Lisa Voigt
Class of 2013

Michael Weiland
Class of 1984

1980	Florence Gurke
1981	Lyman Shepard
1982	Mary Alice Molloy
1983	Robert Irving
1984	Cynthia Maltbie
1985	James Karela
1986	Mary Lou Cardwell
1987	Joe LaRue
1988	Joy Hebert
1989	Art Kruski
1990	Bill Hoffman
1991	Bill Hinchcliff
1992	Louise Haack
1993	Henry Kuehn
1994	Pat Talbot
1995	Dev Bowly, Robert Irving, Bunny Selig, Gloria Wallace
1996	Win Gerulat
1997	Dan Fitzgerald
1998	Margaret Balanoff
1999	Tom Drebenstedt
2000	Chuck Fiori
2001	Diane Lanigan
2002	Alice Schlessinger
2003	Judith Randall
2004	Jack MacDonald
2005	Syma Dodson
2006	Barbara Lancot
2007	Aileen Mandel
2008	Donna Gabanski
2009	Jane Buckwalter
2010	Bobbi Pinkert
2011	Harry Hirsch
2012	Ellen Shubart
2013	Jill Tanz
2014	Mary Jo Hoag
2015	Kathleen Carpenter

Chicago Architecture Foundation Docent Council, April 2016 (Photo: Eric Allix Rogers)